Making Sense of Teaching in Difficult Times

Thinking about teaching in educational terms has become increasingly difficult because of the conceptions of higher education that predominate in both policy and public debate. Framing the benefits of higher education simply as an economic good poses particular difficulties for making educational sense of teaching. Moreover, the assumptions about social mobility, usefulness, and the economic advantages of higher education, upon which these conceptions are based, can no longer be taken for granted.

The chapters in this book all wrestle with understandings of education and teaching experiences in changing global, national, and institutional contexts. They explore questions of difference and privilege, the social transformation of teaching through transforming teachers, contestations of global citizenship and interculturality, learning and sensibilities of self-in-the-world, the relationship between programme content and student decision-making, divergent conceptions of learning in international education, and subject-centred approaches to embodied teaching. The book considers the value of disciplinary tools of analysis in addressing contextual challenges in developing societies, connections between pedagogies, autonomy, and intercultural classrooms, and ways of countering the marketization of higher education through online teaching communities.

This book was originally published as a special issue of *Teaching in Higher Education.*

Penny Jane Burke is Global Innovation Chair of Equity at the University of Newcastle, Australia, where she is Co-Director of the Centre of Excellence for Equity in Higher Education. She is also Professor of Education at Roehampton University, London, UK, where she is Co-Founder and Co-Director of the Paulo Freire Institute-UK, and Research in Inequalities, Societies & Education. She has published extensively in the field of equity in higher education, including *Accessing Education Effectively: Widening Participation* (2002), *The Right to Higher Education: Beyond Widening Participation* (2012), and *Reconceptualising Lifelong Learning: Feminist Interventions* (with Sue Jackson, 2007). She is the Access and Widening Participation Network Co-Convenor for the Society for Research in Higher Education, and Editor of *Teaching in Higher Education.*

Suellen Shay is Associate Professor and Dean in the Centre for Higher Education Development at the University of Cape Town, South Africa. Her career has spanned a range of types of educational development work, including language development, curriculum development, and staff and institutional development. Her research brings the theoretical frameworks of sociology of education to higher education with specific focus on knowledge and curriculum. She is co-editor of *Knowledge-building: Educational Studies in Legitimation Code Theory* (with Karl Maton and Sue Hood, 2015) and has published in a range of higher education journals. She is principle investigator in a multi-institutional research project on undergraduate curriculum reform in South Africa. She is one of the executive editors of *Teaching in Higher Education.*

Making Sense of Teaching in Difficult Times

Edited by

Penny Jane Burke and Suellen Shay

Routledge
Taylor & Francis Group
LONDON AND NEW YORK

First published 2016
by Routledge

2 Park Square, Milton Park, Abingdon, Oxfordshire OX14 4RN
711 Third Avenue, New York, NY 10017

Routledge is an imprint of the Taylor & Francis Group, an informa business

First issued in paperback 2017

British Library Cataloguing in Publication Data
A catalogue record for this book is available from the British Library

ISBN 13: 978-1-138-18490-9 (hbk)
ISBN 13: 978-1-138-30627-1 (pbk)

Typeset in Times
by RefineCatch Limited, Bungay, Suffolk

Publisher's Note
The publisher accepts responsibility for any inconsistencies that may have arisen during the conversion of this book from journal articles to book chapters, namely the possible inclusion of journal terminology.

Contents

Citation Information

The chapters in this book were originally published in *Teaching in Higher Education*, volume 18, issue 7 (October 2013). When citing this material, please use the original page numbering for each article, as follows:

Chapter 1
Difficult times for college students of color: teaching white students about White Privilege provides hope for change
Su L. Boatright-Horowitz, Savannah Frazier, Yvette Harps-Logan and Nathanial Crockett
Teaching in Higher Education, volume 18, issue 7 (October 2013) pp. 698–708

Chapter 2
Teacher as learner: a personal reflection on a short course for South African university educators
Lindsay Clowes
Teaching in Higher Education, volume 18, issue 7 (October 2013) pp. 709–720

Chapter 3
Global citizenship, sojourning students and campus communities
David Killick
Teaching in Higher Education, volume 18, issue 7 (October 2013) pp. 721–735

Chapter 4
Strategies for critiquing global citizenry: undergraduate research as a possible vehicle
Juliet Henderson
Teaching in Higher Education, volume 18, issue 7 (October 2013) pp. 736–747

Chapter 5
Interdisciplinary content, contestations of knowledge and informational transparency in engineering curriculum
Sarah Barnard, Tarek Hassan, Andrew Dainty and Barbara Bagilhole
Teaching in Higher Education, volume 18, issue 7 (October 2013) pp. 748–760

Chapter 6
Chinese students making sense of problem-based learning and Western teaching – pitfalls and coping strategies
Malene Gram, Kirsten Jæger, Junyang Liu, Li Qing and Xiangying Wu
Teaching in Higher Education, volume 18, issue 7 (October 2013) pp. 761–772

Chapter 7
Reframing teaching relationships: from student-centred to subject-centred learning
Julia Hobson and Angus Morrison-Saunders
Teaching in Higher Education, volume 18, issue 7 (October 2013) pp. 773–783

Chapter 8
A heuristic for analysing and teaching literature dealing with the challenges of social justice
Priya Narismulu
Teaching in Higher Education, volume 18, issue 7 (October 2013) pp. 784–796

Chapter 9
The influence of internationalisation and national identity on teaching and assessments in higher education
Jane Vinther and Gordon Slethaug
Teaching in Higher Education, volume 18, issue 7 (October 2013) pp. 797–808

Chapter 10
Online teaching communities within sociology: a counter trend to the marketization of higher education
Nathan Palmer and April M. Schueths
Teaching in Higher Education, volume 18, issue 7 (October 2013) pp. 809–820

Notes on Contributors

Barbara Bagilhole was Emeritus Professor of Social Policy and Equal Opportunities at Loughborough University, UK. Her work helped to challenge the culture of sexism in the construction industry, and demonstrated the extent of discrimination in civil engineering – through male networking, the culture of long working hours, and the use of sexist language – and made the case for change.

Sarah Barnard is a Research Associate in the Department of Civil and Building Engineering at Loughborough University, UK. Her fields of research include gender, higher education, sociology of SET, the private higher education sector, and communications and media.

Su L. Boatright-Horowitz is a Professor in the Department of Psychology at the University of Rhode Island, Kingston, RI, USA. Her research covers antiracism teaching, public perceptions of domestic violence, primate learning and cognition, and undergraduate teaching, research, and programming.

Penny Jane Burke is Global Innovation Chair of Equity at the University of Newcastle, Australia, where she is Co-Director of the Centre of Excellence for Equity in Higher Education. She is also Professor of Education at Roehampton University, London, UK, where she is Co-Founder and Co-Director of the Paulo Freire Institute-UK, and Research in Inequalities, Societies & Education. She has published extensively in the field of equity in higher education. She is the Access and Widening Participation Network Co-Convenor for the Society for Research in Higher Education, and Editor of *Teaching in Higher Education*.

Lindsay Clowes is Head of the Department of Women's and Gender Studies at the University of the Western Cape, Cape Town, South Africa. Drawing on feminist and queer theory as well as discursive psychology, sociology, and critical men's studies, her work problematizes power inequalities and the ways in which human choices are constrained by subject positions structured around biological sex, gender, sexuality, race, and class.

Nathanial Crockett is a graduate student at the University of Rhode Island, Kingston, RI, USA. His research interests include frontier studies, seventeenth-century North America, household archaeology, and foodways.

Andrew Dainty is Professor of Construction Sociology at Loughborough University, UK. His research interests include the resilience of the built environment and the sociology of the construction industry. A renowned expert on the sociologies of construction practice, for the past 20 years his research has focused on the social rules and processes that affect people working as members of project teams.

Savannah Frazier is a Ph.D. student in the Department of Psychology at the University of Rhode Island, Kingston, RI, USA. Her thesis focuses on sociocultural factors related to parents' and caregivers' decisions to vaccinate children against HPV.

Malene Gram is Associate Professor in the Institute for Culture and Global Studies at Aalborg University, Denmark. She is interested in the child's and the young person's voice in family affairs, in light of the sociology of childhood, seeing the child as in the middle of dichotomies of being both competent and vulnerable.

Yvette Harps-Logan is an Associate Professor in the Department of Textiles, Fashion Merchandising and Design at the University of Rhode Island, Kingston, RI, USA. Her research includes fashion merchandising, marketing, and minority consumer behaviour.

Tarek Hassan is Professor of Construction Informatics in the Department of Civil and Building Engineering at Loughborough University, UK. His research interests include advanced ICT in construction, collaborative working environments, information modelling, and e-commerce applications in construction.

Juliet Henderson is based in the Department of History at Oxford Brookes University, UK, where she researches English as a medium for global development processes, critiques of intercultural communication theory, and social, discursive, and cultural drivers of educational change in local universities.

Julia Hobson is Senior Lecturer in the Centre for University Teaching & Learning at Murdoch University, Perth, Australia. She focuses on assisting postgraduate students by developing and delivering seminars and workshops on argumentation, writing, and researching skills. She also works with academic staff to devise intervention workshops that are discipline specific.

Kirsten Jæger is Associate Professor in the Institute for Culture and Global Studies at Aalborg University, Denmark. Her work has been published in journals such as *Nordic Studies in Education, Teaching in Higher Education, Journal of Intercultural Communication,* and *International Journal of Diversity in Organisations, Communities and Nations.*

David Killick is Head of Academic Staff Development in the Centre for Learning and Teaching at Leeds Beckett University, Leeds, UK. He is interested in exploring how we might use student overseas experiences to enhance the home campus and curricula and provide similar journeys towards becoming global citizens.

Junyang Liu is Vice-Chair of the Culture and Communication Department, and a Research Fellow of the Sino-Denmark Joint Research Centre on China and International Relations, at the University of International Relations, Beijing, China.

Angus Morrison-Saunders is Associate Professor in Environmental Assessment at Murdoch University, Perth, Australia. His research focuses on the effectiveness of environmental impact assessment (EIA) and its derivatives such as strategic environmental assessment and sustainability assessment. He is the editor (with Alan Bond and Richard Howitt) of *Sustainability Assessment: Pluralism, Practice and Progress* (Routledge, 2012).

Priya Narismulu is based in the Department of English at the University of Kwa-Zulu Natal, Durban, South Africa. Her research focuses on writing that addresses the apartheid landscape, the medium of English in questions of power and representation, and the politics of home and dislocation.

Nathan Palmer is a Lecturer in Sociology in the Department of Sociology and Anthropology at Georgia Southern University, Statesboro, GA, USA. His research focuses on the sociology of education, race, and ethnicity, environmental sociology, and the scholarship of teaching and learning.

Li Qing is based in the Department of English at the University of International Relations, Beijing, China.

April M. Schueths is Associate Professor of Sociology at Georgia Southern University, Statesboro, GA, USA, and a Licensed Clinical Social Worker. Much of her research focuses on the vulnerabilities of mixed-status couples where she explores the contrast between public perceptions and private realities. She is co-editor of *Living Together, Living Apart: Mixed-Status Families and US Immigration Policy* (2015).

Suellen Shay is Associate Professor and Dean in the Centre for Higher Education Development at the University of Cape Town, South Africa. Her career has spanned a range of types of educational development work, including language development, curriculum development, and staff and institutional development. Her research brings the theoretical frameworks of sociology of education to higher education with specific focus on knowledge and curriculum. She is co-editor of *Knowledge-building: Educational Studies in Legitimation Code Theory* (with Karl Maton and Sue Hood, 2015) and has published in a range of higher education journals. She is principle investigator in a multi-institutional research project on undergraduate curriculum reform in South Africa. She is one of the executive editors of *Teaching in Higher Education*.

Gordon Slethaug is an Adjunct Professor in the Department of English Language and Literature at the University of Waterloo, Canada. He is interested in globalization, semiotics and advertising, contemporary American film and literature, international teaching and learning, and cross-cultural learning. His most recent book is *Hit the Road, Jack: The History and Culture of the Road in America* (ed. with Stacilee Ford, 2012).

Jane Vinther is an Associate Professor in the Department of Language and Communication at the University of Southern Denmark, Odense, Denmark. Her research focuses on applied linguistics, second language acquisition, international teaching and learning, and intercultural communication.

Xiangying Wu is based in the Department of International Economics and Trade at the University of International Relations, Beijing, China.

Acknowledgement

This book is based on an original special issue of *Teaching in Higher Education*, which was produced in response to a call for papers prepared by the journal's former editor, Sue Clegg, and its executive editors, Penny Jane Burke, Cheryl Hunt, Jan Parker, Suellen Shay and Barry Stierer. We worked collaboratively to draft the call, review the submissions (anonymously) and to finally select the seven articles and three essays republished as chapters in this book collection. Our aim was to identify themes of significance that have the potential to push the field and to engage key themes and debates shaping research, conceptions and understanding of teaching in higher education.

Difficult times for college students of color: teaching white students about White Privilege provides hope for change

Su L. Boatright-Horowitz, Savannah Frazier, Yvette Harps-Logan and Nathanial Crockett

Psychology Department, University of Rhode Island, Kingstown, USA

The prevalence of racism and *racial microaggressions* on college campuses is discussed, as well as the negative effects of these occurrences for students of color. An important teaching tool for changing white students' attitudes about racism is presented with an empirical evaluation of its effectiveness. Students read McIntosh's list of White Privileges rating their agreement that each item is a White Privilege in modern US society. Pre-test and post-test questionnaires revealed that white students became more sensitive to issues of racism after this experience. Specifically, these students became more likely to agree that: racism occurs today, racism affects their behavior, they personally benefit from White Privilege, whites in modern society can be viewed as racist, and that they reported that they would be more likely to join student organizations or attend campus events focusing on reducing racism. Regression analyses identified examples of White Privileges with the greatest effect.

Introduction

These are difficult times for persons of color in higher education and in the greater society. Whites in the USA, if not in many countries, tend to view racism as a social problem that has essentially been solved already and they typically believe that racist disparities are confined to the distant historical past (e.g. Bischoping et al. 2001; Boatright-Horowitz 2005). In fact, Norton and Sommers (2011) demonstrated that the majority of white individuals view themselves to be victims of reverse racism more than they view Blacks to be victims of racism. Yet, evidence suggests that racism is still part of the daily lives of persons of color, not only overtly (e.g. Brewster and Rusche 2012) but also in the form of *racial microaggressions,* or 'the brief, commonplace, and daily verbal, behavioral, and environmental slights and indignities directed toward Black Americans, often automatically and unintentionally' (Sue, Capodilupo, and Holder 2008, 329). Racial microaggressions are global occurrences that affect, among others, British Asians (Burdsey 2011). In academic settings, microaggressions may involve a professor mentioning the articulateness of a student of color and expressing surprise, or it may involve white students stereotyping black individuals as criminal, poor, or disadvantaged. Persons of color may feel discomforted or insulted, but they are likely to experience difficulty discussing it because they can expect to be perceived as overreacting by whites to minor or nonexistent racist offenses. Lowe, Okubo, and Reilly (2012, 193) described the effects of the trauma that can be caused by encounters with racism, as well as the secondary trauma that resulted when others 'minimized, dismissed, or blamed the individual for the racism they encountered'. In some cases (e.g. professor and student), there may be power disparities that make the situation even more complicated. Thus, these are particularly difficult times for students of color on college campuses because the social climate is still racist and many whites fail to acknowledge this problem. We discuss occurrences of racism and microaggressions as they occur on university and college campuses today, as well as the potential negative effects on students of color. We also present a teaching tool for reducing racism in white students, providing empirical evidence of its effectiveness. Although our focus is primarily on racism as it affects black or African American students on college campuses in the USA today, this information may be generalized to university or college students of other non-white ethnicities, as well as students of color from other countries.

Racism on university and college campuses

The existence of racism (e.g. Brewster and Rusche 2012), particularly as it occurs on predominantly white college campuses, is unequivocal. McCarthy (1993) described incidences of overt racism on college campuses, including physical beatings of black individuals, cross-burnings, mock slave auctions with the 'slaves' wearing afro wigs, 'jungle parties' in which white fraternity brothers wore black body paint and rings in their noses. Schwitzer et al. (1999) reported that African American students tend to experience predominantly white campuses as 'hostile' and 'foreign', also indicating that this uncomfortable day-to-day feeling of being socially distanced was an unexpected experience for them. One student stated that she '... always felt isolated'. 'When you enter a room, you look for another Black person and you always speak' (p. 192). Furthermore, African American students reported a sense of intimidation when they contacted faculty outside of the classroom (e.g. 'Some professors feel I need help because I am Black'.) Bunzel (1991) conducted an investigation of the experiences of students at Stanford University and reported that 95% of blacks felt that they did not fit into the campus community. More than 70% of these black participants said that they felt that they were viewed as lacking academic competence by faculty and others on campus. McClelland and Auster (1990) reported that white students desire significantly greater distance from black students than vice versa, pointing out that white students experience campus climates as relatively calm, whereas black students are necessarily more attuned to covert racial tensions. Vaccaro (2010) used qualitative analyses to investigate the campus climate for women and persons of minority status at a predominantly white college campus in New England. Open-ended questionnaire items resulted in hostile, anti-diversity, sexist, and insulting responses (e.g. 'Students really do not care about race or sexual identity... administrative suits like the ones that came up with this shit survey do!') and when asked about what they like about the campus, 'Hot blonde girls, tons of money spent for landscaping campus, classes not hard' (pp. 209–210). Vaccaro concluded that these were more than just immature comments from undergraduate students because hostility about diversity issues occurred for graduate students, faculty and staff, particularly males. On another college campus, Sydell and Nelson

(2000) reported that 65% of black students reported experiences of verbal racial harassment, while about 50% of white students admitted to exhibiting open dislike (e.g. name calling, physical violence, negative facial expressions) toward others because of their race. We can only conclude that racism, both overt and covert, continues to occur on college campuses today.

The effects of racism on students of color

It is well known that exposure to racism and perceptions of racist events serve as strong predictors of psychological stress in black Americans (e.g. Pieterse et al. 2010). Even covert forms of racism are detrimental to students, in part because they are subtle and difficult for black students to discuss with others (Bunzel 1991). When black students attempt to describe their feelings of discomfort, exclusion, and alienation at predominantly white campuses, they risk being viewed as 'complainers' or 'paranoids' who are simply seeking illegitimate special favors (McClelland and Auster 1990). Many attempts to discuss issues of privilege and covert racism with white individuals tend to be met with a wall of indifference (or even hostility) that is difficult to penetrate. Smith, Hung, and Franklin (2011) referred to the consequences of racism in black male college students as Racial Battle Fatigue. Chao, Mallinckrodt, and Meifen (2012) studied archival records for black or African American college students, most of whom were located on predominantly white campuses, and reported that perceived racial discrimination was associated with a broad range of co-occurring presenting problems, including academic, interpersonal, and psychological/emotional issues. Scholars agree that the effects of racial discrimination are psychologically harmful and cumulative. Sue et al. (2008) pointed out the need to proactively provide effective therapies for victims of racial microaggressions. This problem is serious. Black students on our college campuses are vulnerable to racial violence, exposed to psychological stressors in the form of careless racial comments and jokes (McClelland and Auster 1990), and they are embedded in systematically racist academic institutions with few black faculty and administrators (Jayakumar et al. 2009).

Can educational interventions reduce racism?

There is hope for students of color. Research has shown that social climates on college campuses can have a significant impact on the academic success of African American college students. Schwitzer et al. (1999) reported that warmer (i.e. less racist) institutional climates are associated with higher graduation rates for black students. Yet, McClelland and Auster (1990) reported that there were no significant differences across class levels (i.e. seniors were no different from freshmen), and they concluded that the years that students spent on college campuses had little or no effect on racist attitudes in white students. On the other hand, using meta-analysis, Denson (2009) concluded that institutional effort can result in measurable changes. According to Denson (2009; adapted from Dovidio et al. 2004), racism can be reduced through intentional use of curricular and co-curricular activities that involve enlightenment and/or inter-group contact. Personal enlightenment is a result of expanding an individual's content-based knowledge of other groups or altering the individual's perspective about relations with others. It therefore seems reasonable to suggest that exposure to examples of racism can facilitate personal enlightenment about racism, which can be enhanced by inter-group discussions about White Privilege.

A teaching tool for reducing racism

For many years, the large General Psychology course (typically, more than 700 students) at our institution has included a course module with class discussions of White Privilege (McIntosh 1988). The effectiveness of this course module has been assessed periodically (e.g. Boatright-Horowitz 2005), including replication with a yoked control group on a different campus (unpublished data). In 2009, the use of this course module resulted in an award from the Society for the Teaching of Psychology for infusing diversity into teaching. Based on class discussions with thousands of students over the years, it seemed clear that exposure to McIntosh's (1988) list of White Privileges was a major factor in changing white students' attitudes about racism. In 1988, Peggy McIntosh published a list of the many privileges in daily life that are the direct result of being white. Reading this list of White Privileges can increase awareness of the prevalence of racism in modern society, as well as the ways in which it is manifested. White Privileges include situations such as, 'I can go shopping alone most of the time, pretty well assured that I will not be followed or harassed' and 'I can be sure that if I need legal or medical help, my race will not work against me'. Basically, these are unearned privileges in the daily lives of white individuals who typically remain unaware that they have benefits unavailable to others in society. As one of Jackson and Heckman's (2002) students stated, being '... White is normal to a lot of people, so we don't really have to think about it because we're not forced to think about it' (p. 442). In an investigation of white student reactions to a racial hate crime on campus, Jackson and Heckman's (2002) students reported that they had witnessed overt acts of racism on campus, yet they still viewed racism to be something that occurred in the past, without understanding its relevance to their own lives. Bunzel (1991) studied racial relations at Stanford University and reported that most white students said that they were tired of hearing about racism. According to Sydell and Nelson (2000, 629), white college students often view black students as self-segregating and white students tend to think that 'Black students should de-emphasize their ethnicity in order to fit into White society', without acknowledging that 'fitting in' means accepting the *status quo* of White Privilege. Jackson and Heckman (2002) commented that whites in modern society wear rose-colored glasses regarding racism and that '... many Whites these days want non-Whites to have rose-colored glasses, too ...' (p. 448).

Whites in modern society are socialized to unconsciously view the world through the lens of racism, without awareness of the privileges associated with being white. According to Hansman et al. (1999, 16) '... a deeper understanding at the cultural and institutional levels is necessary in order to effectively confront the powerful and subtle forms of racism that exist today'. We suggest that inclusion of discussions of White Privilege in the educational curriculum can help educators achieve this goal. Although McIntosh's (1988) paper is still widely read more than 20 years after it was originally written, it has not become part of mainstream survey courses at colleges and universities (e.g. General Psychology, Introduction to Sociology). Yet, it appears to have a measurable effect on reducing racism in white students and its importance is evidenced by more than 100 citations in the *Web of Science*, with about half occurring during the last 10 years, as well as more than 1500 citations for papers that cite this original work.

Therefore, we decided to examine student reactions to the list of White Privileges, assessing student levels of agreement with each item on the list and measuring the impact of this information on the racist attitudes and beliefs of white students. Yet, we need to apologize here because our primary focus in this research involved changing the attitudes of white students about White Privilege. Unfortunately, this emphasis is consistent with the nature of White Privilege itself – attention is given to white students as a function of position in society and skin color. We hope that there is justification for this because the primary goal was to reduce racism.

Method

Subjects

Participants were 274 students enrolled in a General Psychology course at a northeastern university. Sixty were students of color (e.g. African American, Arab, Native American) and 214 were students who identified themselves as white, Caucasian, or European American. Students took part in this research to earn a small amount of extra credit in this course.

Procedure

An online survey system presented McIntosh's (1988) list of White Privileges and asked students to rate their levels of agreement that each item is a White Privilege in modern society. Pre-test and post-test questions assessed changes in students' attitudes about racism as a function of exposure to the White Privilege list. The Crowne and Marlowe (1960) test was used to assess whether participants responded to questionnaire items in a socially desirable way (i.e. to make themselves look good).

Results

For the students of color, we were particularly interested in which items in the privilege list were most applicable to their lives (i.e. which items still hold true more than 20 years after the list was first published). The highest levels of agreement occurred for items related to the quality of life at home, while shopping or traveling, and in obtaining career advice (Table 1). Two of these items were also among those with the highest ratings of agreement for the white students, specifically items involving freedom from harassment while shopping and the accessibility of professional mentors. Overall, white students showed significantly higher levels of agreement with the list of White Privileges than the students of color ($t = 4.95$, $df = 272$, $p = 0.000$; for white students: Mean $= 6.62$, SD $= 1.47$, $N = 214$ and for students of color: Mean $= 5.57$, SD $= 1.37$, $N = 60$). For the six students who self-identified as black or African American, overall ratings of agreement with the items in the list of White Privileges appeared to be comparable to those of the students of color (Mean $= 5.63$, SD $= 1.21$, $N = 6$), although there were too few for quantitative comparisons.

Table 1. Items in McIntosh's (1988) White Privilege list with the highest ratings of agreement, based on a 10-point scale.

	Mean	SD	*N*
Students of color			
'If I should need to move, I can be pretty sure of renting or purchasing housing in an area which I can afford and in which I would want to live'.	6.94	2.43	60
'I can go shopping alone most of the time, pretty well assured that I will not be followed or harassed'.	6.90	2.67	60
'I can travel alone or with my spouse without expecting embarrassment or hostility in those who deal with us'.	6.58	2.53	60
'I can be pretty sure of finding people who would be willing to talk with me and advise me about my next steps, professionally'.	6.52	2.76	60
'I can be pretty sure that my neighbors in such a location will be neutral or pleasant to me'.	6.50	2.27	60
White students			
'I can easily buy posters, post-cards, picture books, greeting cards, dolls, toys and children's magazines featuring people of my race'.	7.87	2.45	214
'I can go shopping alone most of the time, pretty well assured that I will not be followed or harassed'.	7.80	2.33	214
'I can turn on the television or open to the front page of the paper and see people of my race widely represented'.	7.78	2.26	214
'I can be sure that if I need legal or medical help, my race will not work against me'.	7.78	2.54	214
'I can be pretty sure of finding people who would be willing to talk with me and advise me about my next steps, professionally'.	7.59	2.42	214

Note: Mean levels of agreement with these items for the students who identified themselves as black or African American ($N=7$) ranged from 5.00 to 7.86, and were comparable to those of the students of color.

Seven questionnaire items assessed participants' attitudes about racism in the pre- and post-tests (Table 2). Participants' responses to these items were not correlated with scores on the Crowne–Marlowe test of social desirability, indicating that these data were not the result of participants responding to presenting themselves positively. For the white students, repeated measures ANOVAs revealed that mean responses to six of these questionnaire items were significantly higher in the post-test, compared to the pre-test. Using a 10-point scale to indicate how much racism exists in US society today, white students responded with higher levels after exposure to McIntosh's list of White Privileges ($F=20.95$, df $=1$, $p=0.000$, effect size: Cohen's $d=0.31$). Similarly, there was a significant increase when asked if racism affected their own behavior ($F=3.47$, df $=1$, $p=0.064$, effect size: Cohen's $d=0.11$). Admissions that they experienced White Privilege also increased significantly ($F=52.47$, df $=1$, $p=0.000$, effect size: Cohen's $d=0.47$), as did reports that other people are likely to view them as racist ($F=12.48$, df $=1$, $p=0.000$, effect size: Cohen's $d=0.21$). White student agreement that whites in today's society can be viewed as racist increased significantly ($F=12.48$, df $=1$, $p=0.000$, effect size: Cohen's $d=0.21$) and there was a significant increase in white student agreement that they would join student organizations or attend campus events to reduce racism ($F=8.65$, df $=1$, $p=0.004$, effect size: Cohen's $d=0.15$). On the other hand, there

Table 2. Changes in attitudes about racism as a function of exposure to items in McIntosh's (1988) White Privilege list, based on 10-point scales.

	Pre-test			Post-test		
	Mean	SD	*N*	Mean	SD	*N*
White students						
'Using a scale ranging from "1" (not at all racist) to "10" (extremely racist), indicate how much racism exists in US society today'.	5.53	2.05	214	6.14	1.82	214
'Racism affects the way I behave with others'.	3.16	2.21	214	3.41	2.17	214
'I have personally experienced many privileges based on my race or ethnicity'.	4.29	2.75	214	5.44	2.77	214
'Other people are likely to view me as racist'.	2.19	1.70	214	2.59	2.02	214
'In general, Whites in US society can be viewed as racist'.	4.79	2.33	214	5.19	2.36	214
'How likely are you to join student organizations or participate in campus events that focus on reducing racism?'	4.00	2.40	214	4.37	2.67	214
'Racism is still a major problem in the USA today'.	6.35	2.12	214	6.35	2.10	214
Students of color						
'Using a scale ranging from "1" (not at all racist) to "10" (extremely racist), indicate how much racism exists in US society today'.	6.15	2.40	60	6.68	1.94	60
'Racism affects the way I behave with others'.	4.77	2.92	60	4.67	2.83	60
'I have personally experienced many privileges based on my race or ethnicity'.	4.08	2.72	60	3.98	2.50	60
'Other people are likely to view me as racist'.	2.22	1.95	60	2.60	2.08	60
'In general, Whites in US society can be viewed as racist'.	4.93	2.46	60	5.57	2.32	60
'How likely are you to join student organizations or participate in campus events that focus on reducing racism?'	5.82	2.90	60	5.73	2.90	60
'Racism is still a major problem in the US today'.	7.57	1.89	60	7.13	2.10	60

was no significant change in white student agreement with the statement that racism is still a major problem in the US today ($F=0.00$, df $=1$, $p=1.00$), perhaps due to a ceiling effect because this item had already resulted in the highest mean level of agreement of all of pre-test items.

Attitude change for each participant was assessed using ratio measures for each questionnaire item about modern racism (i.e. post-tests divided by pre-tests). Regression analyses were used to determine how much each item in McIntosh's list of White Privileges contributed to these attitude changes. Although it was problematic to use all 50 items in McIntosh's list as potential predictor variables, this was exploratory research that could guide decisions about which White Privilege items should be selected for discussions during limited class periods. These data met assumptions of multicollinearity, normality, Cook's distance, and leverage. Heteroscedasticity and Mahalanobis testing appeared to be problematic, probably due to the cumulative effects of reading about White Privileges (i.e. mean attitude change for the second half of the list (Mean $=6.67$, SD $=1.56$) was greater than for the first half of the list (Mean $=6.57$, SD $=1.51$), with the difference approaching significance for the white students ($t = -1.69$, df $=213$, $p = 0.093$). In these analyses, only two items appeared to predict participant responses to the item regarding how much racism exists in modern society. The statements that 'I can go shopping alone most of the time, pretty well assured that I will not be followed or harassed' ($b = 0.20$, $t(192) = 1.99$, $p = 0.048$) and 'I can chose blemish cover or bandages in "flesh" color and have them more or less match my skin' ($b = 0.23$, $t(192) = 1.96$, $p = 0.052$) appeared to contribute significantly ($F = 1.44$, df $= 50$, $p = 0.05$; $R^2 = 0.20$). Acknowledgment by participants that they have personally experienced White Privilege was associated with 'I can be late to a meeting without having the lateness reflect on my race', ($b = -0.32$, $t(192) = -2.93$, $p = 0.00$) and 'If a traffic cop pulls me over or if the IRS audits my tax return, I can be sure I haven't been singled out because of my race' ($b = -0.19$, $t(192) = -1.88$, $p = 0.06$; $F = 1.56$, df $= 50$, $p = 0.02$; $R^2 = 0.32$), although responses to the former item were significantly correlated with Crowne–Marlowe scores of social desirability.

Awareness that other people may view them as racist was significantly associated with six items on MecIntosh's list of White Privileges, specifically 'I can if I wish arrange to be in the company of people of my race most of the time' ($b = -0.21$, $t(192) = -2.18$, $p = 0.03$), 'I can be sure that my children will be given curricular materials that testify to the existence of their race' ($b = 0.20$, $t(292) = 2.06$, $p = 0.04$), 'I can be pretty sure of finding people who would be willing to talk with me and advise me about my next steps, professionally' ($b = 0.25$, $t(192) = 2.19$, $p = 0.03$), 'I can think over many options, social, political, imaginative or professional, without asking whether a person of my race would be accepted or allowed to do what I want to do' ($b = -0.40$, $t(192) = -3.05$, $p = 0.00$), 'I can choose public accommodation without fearing that people of my race cannot get in or will be mistreated in the places I have chosen' ($b = 0.32$, $t(192) = 2.65$, $p = 0.00$), and 'I can be sure that if I need legal or medical help, my race will not work against me' ($b = -0.23$, $t(192) = -1.88$, $p = 0.06$; ($F = 1.44$, df $= 50$, $p = 0.05$; $R^2 = 0.31$). Attitude change for the remaining four questionnaire items assessing racism were not associated with predictor variables (all $p > 0.05$).

Discussion

One goal of the present research was to identify which of the White Privileges on McIntosh's list were associated with the highest levels of agreement in college students. Students of color tend to view White Privilege to be relevant to aspects of their lives that involve finding housing with friendly neighbors, traveling, shopping, and finding professional mentors. In other words, these are the types of situations in which students of color expect to encounter racism. It is encouraging that white students gave the highest ratings to two of the same items (i.e. shopping and finding professional mentors). The most surprising finding in this research was that white students had significantly higher levels of agreement with items on the list of White Privileges than the students of color. This may be related to diversity within the group of students identified as students of color (i.e. students whose ethnicities are not likely to afford them White Privileges, specifically, Native American, Arab, Indian, etc.). Therefore, it would be helpful to replicate this research in the future with more African American or black participants, a type of study that tends to be difficult to conduct on our predominantly white college campus.

The most important finding in this research was empirical evidence that exposure to McIntosh's (1988) list of White Privileges can result in attitude changes about racism in white students. After reading and rating their levels of agreement with items on this list, white students responded with higher ratings about how much racism exists in modern US society and they were more likely to acknowledge that racism affects their own behavior. They were more likely to admit that they personally benefit from these privileges. These students were also more likely to acknowledge that other people may view them as racist and that whites in modern society tend to be racist. Finally, these students were more likely to indicate that they would join student organizations or attend campus events to reduce racism. Effect sizes were small, but this may be common with antiracism interventions (Boatright-Horowitz 2005; Morelli and Spencer 2000), possibly due to individual differences in student openness about issues of racism or the result of differences in levels of privilege in the backgrounds of the white students. Pedersen et al. (2011) suggested that white students who do not perceive themselves as having privileged backgrounds may be more resistant to antiracism teaching. This is consistent with our own observations in a qualitative analysis of college students' cognitive and emotional reactions after they learned about White Privilege (Boatright-Horowitz, Marraccini, and Harps-Logan 2011), Yet, whites who view themselves as lacking privileges still do not have to experience the effects of racism in their daily lives.

We were also interested in identifying the specific items in the list of White Privileges that could be presented most effectively in classroom discussions, given the limitations on class time in introductory survey courses. Therefore, we used exploratory regression analyses to identify which items in the list predicted attitude changes. Although it is problematic to test 50 variables in this type of analysis, future research can focus more specifically on the White Privilege items identified as effective. There were two items in the list that significantly predicted the levels of racism in modern US society reported by white students. These items involved the opportunity to shop without racially based harassment and the purchase of bandages and blemish colors to match skin color, relatively concrete examples of White Privilege that are within the experiences of many white students. Acknowledgment by white students that they have personally experienced White Privilege was predicted by two items (i.e. 'I can be late to a meeting without having the lateness reflect on my race' and 'If a traffic cop pulls me over or if the IRS audits my tax return, I can be sure I haven't been singled out because of my race'). Again, these are typically within the experiences of white college students because they are likely to have been late to meetings, stopped by traffic cops, and many students have filled out tax forms. There were six items on the list of White Privilege that predicted whether white students acknowledged that other people might view them as racist (i.e. the opportunity to associate primarily with other people of one's own ethnicity, whether one's children are given curricular materials that reflect their ethnicities, obtaining professional assistance with careers, being allowed social, political, imaginative, and professional opportunities, using public accommodations, and acquiring medical or legal assistance). One interpretation of this finding is that white students believe they will be perceived as benefiting from White Privilege in these types of situations; therefore, they expect resentment from persons of color who may view them as racist. Yet, it may be beneficial for white students to have an expectation that they might be viewed as racist, particularly if they understand the underlying reasons for such perceptions. This realization may make white students more sensitive about the types of comments and jokes that can hurt or offend the people around them, as well as more aware of social injustices in modern society.

In conclusion, exposure to McIntosh's (1988) list of White Privileges appears to have a significant impact on white students' attitudes about racism. We encourage college instructors to teach students about White Privilege, particularly in introductory survey courses because the denial of White Privilege perpetuates racial discrimination. We further suggest that omitting this topic from the college curriculum is itself a manifestation of White Privilege. Providing students with the opportunity to examine the list of White Privileges, rating their levels of agreement with each item, facilitates processing of this information in enough depth to impact attitudes about racism. Finally, we would like to comment that the list of White Privileges identified by McIntosh covers a wide range of human activities, including housing, shopping, obtaining medical and legal assistance, career-training, travel, television viewing, child safety, and academic curricula. All of these various human activities and contexts are impacted by racism for persons of color and it is important for our white students to acknowledge this concept. After all, the ultimate White Privilege is to experience freedom from racism in all aspects of one's daily life and we wish that *all* of our students will eventually have this freedom, but effort and effective educational tools are necessary to achieve this goal.

References

Bischoping, K., C. Dodds, M. Jama, C. Johnson, A. Kalmin, and K. Reid. 2001. "Talking About Silence: Reflections on "Race" in a University Course on Genocide." *Reflective Practice* 2: 155–169. doi:10.1080/14623940124838.

Boatright-Horowitz, S. L. 2005. "Teaching Antiracism in a Large Introductory Psychology Class: A Course Module and Its Evaluation." *Journal of Black Studies* 36 (1): 34–51. doi:10.1177/0021934704266508.

Boatright-Horowitz, S. L., M. Marraccini, and Y. Harps-Logan. 2011. "Teaching Antiracism: College Students' Emotional and Cognitive Reactions to Learning about White Privilege." Paper presented at the 2011 Pedagogy of Privilege conference, Denver, CO.

Brewster, Z., and S. N. Rusche. 2012. "Quantitative Evidence of the Continuing Significance of Race: Tableside Racism in Full-Service Restaurants." *Journal of Black Studies* 43 (4): 359–384. doi:10.1177/0021934711433310.

Bunzel, J. H. 1991. "Black and White at Stanford." *Public Interest* 105: 61–77. http://www.nationalaffairs.com/public_interest/detail/black-and-white-at-stanford.

Burdsey, D. 2011. "That Joke Isn't Funny Anymore: Racial Microaggressions, Color-Blind Ideology and the Mitigation of Racism in English Men's First-Class Cricket." *Sociology of Sport Journal* 28 (3): 261–283. http://0-journals.humankinetics.com.helin.uri.edu/AcuCustom/SiteName/Documents/DocumentItem/01_ssj%2028_3%20Burdsey_2010_0112.pdf.

Chao, R., B. Mallinckrodt, and W. Meifen. 2012. "Co-Occurring Presenting Problems in African American College Clients Reporting Racial Discrimination Distress." *Professional Psychology: Research & Practice* 43 (3): 199–207. doi:10.1037/a0027861.

Crowne, D. P., and D. Marlowe. 1960. "A New Scale of Social Desirability Independent of Psychopathology." *Journal of Consulting Psychology* 24: 349–354. doi:10.1037/h0047358.

Denson, N. 2009. "Do Curricular and Cocurricular Diversity Activities Influence Racial Bias? A Meta-Analysis." *Review of Educational Research* 79 (2): 805–838. doi:10.3102/0034654309331551.

Dovidio, J. F., S. L. Gaertner, T. L. Stewart, V. M. Esses, M. Vergert, and G. Hodson. 2004. "From Intervention to Outcome: Processes in the Reduction of Bias." In *Education Programs for Improving Intergroup Relations*, edited by W. G. Stephan, and W. P. Vogt, 243–265. New York: Teachers College Press.

Hansman, C. A., L. Spencer, D. Grant, and M. Jackson. 1999. "Beyond Diversity: Dismantling Barriers in Education." *Journal of Instructional Psychology* 26 (1): 16. http://www.projectinnovation.biz/jip_2006.html.

Jackson II, R., and S. M. Heckman. 2002. "Perceptions of White Identity and White Liability: An Analysis of White Student Responses to a College Campus Racial Hate Crime." *Journal of Communication* 52 (2): 434–450. doi:10.1111/j.1460-2466.2002.tb02554.x.

Jayakumar, U. M., T. C. Howard, W. R. Allen, and J. C. Han. 2009. "Racial Privilege in the Professoriate: An Exploration of Campus Climate, Retention, and Satisfaction." *The Journal of Higher Education* 80 (5): 538–563. doi:10.1353/jhe.0.0063.

Lowe, S., Y. Okubo, and M. F. Reilly. 2012. "A Qualitative Inquiry into Racism, Trauma, and Coping: Implications for Supporting Victims of Racism." *Professional Psychology: Research & Practice* 43 (3): 190–198. doi:10.1037/a0026501.

McCarthy, C. 1993. "Racial Resentment in American Higher Education: The Campus Scene in the '90s." *Social Alternatives* 12 (1): 31–35. http://socialalternatives.com/.

McClelland, K. E., and C. J. Auster. 1990. "Public Platitudes and Hidden Tensions Racial Climates at Predominantly White Liberal Arts Colleges." *Journal of Higher Education* 61 (6): 607–642. doi:10.2307/1981988.

McIntosh, P. 1988. *White Privilege and Male Privilege: A Personal Account of Coming to See Correspondences through Work in Women's Studies* (Working Paper No. 189). Wellesley, MA: Wellesley College, Center for Research on Women.

Morelli, P., and M. Spencer. 2000. "Use and Support of Multicultural and Antiracist Education: Research-Informed Interdisciplinary Social Work Practice." *Social Work* 45 (2): 166–175. doi:10.1093/sw/45.2.166.

Norton, M. I., and S. R. Sommers. 2011. "Whites See Racism as a Zero-Sum Game That They Are Now Losing." *Perspectives on Psychological Science* 6 (3): 215–218. doi:10.1177/1745691611406922.

Pedersen, A., I. Walker, Y. Paradies, and B. Guerin. 2011. "How to Cook Rice: A Review of Ingredients for Teaching Anti-Prejudice." *Australian Psychologist* 46 (1): 55–63. doi:10.1111/j.1742-9544.2010.00015.x.

Pieterse, A. L., R. T. Carter, S. A. Evans, and R. A. Walter. 2010. "An Exploratory Examination of the Associations among Racial and Ethnic Discrimination, Racial Climate, and Trauma-Related Symptoms in a College Student Population." *Journal of Counseling Psychology* 57 (3): 255–263. doi:10.1037/a0020040.

Schwitzer, A. M., O. T. Griffin, J. R. Ancis, and C. R. Thomas. 1999. "Social Adjustment Experiences of African American College Students." *Journal of Counseling and Development* 77 (2): 189–197. doi:10.1002/j.1556-6676.1999.tb02439.x.

Smith, W. A., M. Hung, and J. D. Franklin. 2011. "Racial Battle Fatigue and the MisEducation of Black Men: Racial Microaggressions, Societal Problems, and Environmental Stress." *Journal of Negro Education* 80 (1): 63–82. http://www.journalnegroed.org/winter2011.html.

Sue, D. W., C. M. Capodilupo, and A. B. Holder. 2008. "Racial Microaggressions in the Life Experience of Black Americans." *Professional Psychology: Research & Practice* 39 (3): 329–336. doi:10.1037/0735-7028.39.3.329.

Sue, D. W., K. L. Nadal, C. M. Capodilupo, A. I. Lin, G. C. Torino, and D. P. Rivera. 2008. "Racial Microaggressions Against Black Americans: Implications for Counseling. "*Journal of Counseling & Development* 86 (3): 330–338. doi:10.1002/j.1556-6678.2008.tb00517.x.

Sydell, E. J., and E. S. Nelson. 2000. "Modern Racism on Campus: A Survey of Attitudes and Perceptions." *Social Science Journal* 37 (4): 627–636. doi:10.1016/S0362-3319(00)00105-1.

Vaccaro, A. 2010. "What Lies Beneath Seemingly Positive Campus Climate Results: Institutional Sexism, Symbolic Racism, and Male Hostility Toward Equity Initiatives." *Journal of Equity and Excellence in Education* 43 (2): 202–215. doi:10.1080/10665680903520231.

Teacher as learner: a personal reflection on a short course for South African university educators

Lindsay Clowes

Women's and Gender Studies Department, University of the Western Cape, Cape Town, South Africa

Higher education is understood to play a critical role in ongoing processes of social transformation in post-apartheid South Africa through the production of graduates who are critical and engaged citizens. A key challenge is that institutions of higher education are themselves implicated in reproducing the very hierarchies they hope to transform. In this paper, I reflect critically on my experiences of a course aimed at transforming teaching through transforming teachers. In this paper, I foreground my own positionality as a white female educator as I draw on feminist theorising to reflect on my experiences as a learner in the Community, Self and Identity course. I suggest that we need to teach in ways that are more cognisant of the complexities of the constraints on personal freedom in the past if we are to contribute to the development of social justice in the future.

Introduction

The South African context of higher education is one in which global debates around the role of the humanities, impact of market fundamentalism, the corporatisation of the university, role of emerging technologies and so on are complicated by legacies of struggle that continue to be expressed through inequalities structured around gender, sexuality, class, race, ethnicity, generation, disability and religion etc., alongside constitutional and ethical imperatives to challenge such inequalities. South African institutions of higher education have employed a range of strategies and approaches aimed at contributing towards the social transformation eliminating these inequalities requires. An important element of this has been to acknowledge that institutions themselves are implicated in reproducing the very hierarchies that must be challenged. For South African educators, this is a complex and difficult terrain: if we are to develop graduates who are critical and engaged citizens we need to start with ourselves. One innovative response to this has been a collaboration between the Directorate of Teaching and Learning at the University of the Western Cape and the University of Stellenbosch's Centre for Teaching and Learning in the development of a module offered to teachers in institutions of higher education. Underpinning the module was the understanding that the production of graduates who were critically aware citizens required the transformation of teaching practices through the transformation of teachers. In this paper, I reflect on my experiences and learnings as an educator turned student in the *Community, Self and Identity* (CSI) course of 2010 by drawing on feminist theorising acknowledging the blurring of distinct lines between the personal and the professional, and that foregrounds my positionality as a feminist, and as a white, female educator implicated in the hierarchies alluded to above.

South African landscapes of higher education

Challenges facing educators globally take on very particular flavours in South African contexts of higher education. The transition from a white supremacist regime to a democratic state with a constitutional imperative towards equity has meant that every South African is confronted daily by the challenge of living 'beyond the destructive appeals of their exclusionary pasts' (Soudien 2012, 4). Like other citizens, South African educators are presented, individually and collectively, from one moment to the next, with multiple opportunities from which to 'imagine a future in which the value of being human is primary' (Soudien 2012, 4). South African education – and higher education in particular – is central to this act of imagining, through providing the intellectual insights, motivation and tools to 'trouble' received knowledges that essentialise identities and the corresponding inequalities built around race, gender, sexuality, class, religion and other salient subject locations. For Crain Soudien (2012, 4), South African education represents a 'unique' opportunity 'for rethinking the questions of 'how-to-be' and how human beings can 'be-together' in ways that few other societies in the world are doing'.

Confronting apartheid legacies of inequalities has been central to the development of higher education policy in post-apartheid South Africa (see Lange and Singh 2010), most recently by the appointment of the Oversight Committee on the Transformation of South African Universities (DHET 2013; see also the *Mail and Guardian* Special Report 2013). Formed on the recommendation of a Ministerial Committee on Transformation and Social Cohesion and the Elimination of Discrimination in Public Higher Education that insisted that 'discrimination, in particular with regard to racism and sexism, is pervasive' in institutions of higher education (DHET 2008, 13), the Oversight Committee is tasked with advising the Minister of Higher Education with regard to elimination of 'racism, sexism and other forms of unfair discrimination' in public universities (DHET 2013, 2). The Oversight Committee emerges out of a long-standing policy emphasis on the centrality of redress and equity in terms of higher education's role in social and political transformation, alongside recognition that the educational system itself needs to be transformed in order to fulfil its 'immense potential to contribute to the consolidation of democracy and social justice' (CHE 2000, 25 cited in the Draft National Plan 2001, 5). The tensions and fractures permeating the complex terrain within which South African educators operate are exemplified by responses to this initiative: While some academics have welcomed it as a 'long-overdue move', others insist the committee to be nothing more than 'a permanent commissariat to police transformation that will no doubt massacre some universities' (*Daily Maverick* January 31 2013), and still others warn that 'regulatory overkill threatens academic autonomy' (*Business Day* live January 31 2013).

Local initiatives

It is within this uneven and contested terrain that institutional processes of self-conscious reflection on the scholarship and practices of teaching and learning have seen the establishment of structures aimed at deepening transformation within institutions of higher education. In the Western Cape, the Centre for Teaching and Learning was set up at the University of Stellenbosch (US) in 2003 and the Directorate of Teaching and Learning established in 2008 at the University of the Western Cape (UWC). Working together on a 'cross-institutional collaborative teaching and learning project promoting inclusivity', these two structures agreed that the overall policy objectives of developing a more critical and transformative system of higher education were constrained by the 'continuing impact of apartheid-designed segregated higher education institutions and lack of imaginative attention to issues of difference in teaching and learning' as well as a shortage of appropriately equipped educators (Bozalek 2009, 4–5). The 'disjuncture' between 'policy intentions and the actual experiences of students and staff in the higher education sector' (Bozalek 2009, 4–5) combined to limit the development of graduates as 'critical and responsible citizens who contribute to the social and economic well-being of society' (Development of Graduate Attributes at UWC nd:1–2). In order to begin to address this disjuncture, UWC and US collaborated in the development of a module aimed at developing the skills of higher education educators in order to better equip them to produce alumni who were 'engaged, committed and accountable agents of social good [who] aspire to contribute to social justice and care, appreciative of the complexity of historical contexts and societal conditions' (Development of Graduate Attributes at UWC nd:1–2).

The CSI course of 2010 was taught by a team of educators from UWC's Directorate of Teaching and Learning (assisted by a digital media expert), the US Centre for Teaching and Learning, and the US Department of Psychology. Advertised nationally, the course aimed to align the development of educators with the aspirations for graduates articulated in the Charter of Graduate Attributes. Its objectives, as articulated in the course outline, were informed by the belief that developing teachers and transforming teaching practices were central to the development of graduates as critically aware citizens. The teachers who enrolled as learners were to be encouraged to reflect critically on 'notions of community, self and identity in relation to difference and social inclusion in higher education', to 'deepen [their] learning about diversity and difference', enhance their reflexivity and capacity for 'critical questioning as a helpful resource in higher education', to reduce isolation and build community, deepen familiarity with electronic and participatory technologies for creating and sustaining communities as well as to engage with the scholarship of teaching and learning (Course Outline 2010). It was hoped that the experiential and theoretical learning employed by the module would empower participants to '[i]nterrogate the notions of 'social justice', 'community', 'self' and 'identity' through examining own experience [sic], engaging with literature on the topic and sharing ideas across disciplines and institutions with collaborative partners' (Course Outline 2010).

The overall aim of the module, as I understood it, was to engage teachers in critically reflecting on their own prior knowledges and social locations with a view to deepening their understanding of ways in which educators are themselves 'implicated within the social and pedagogical narrative...themselves carriers of troubled knowledge' (Jansen 2009, 258). This seemed, to me, to be an opportunity to raise awareness 'of the full possibility of what it means to be human', an awareness that is only complete 'when the learnt prejudices and false certainties of race and gender and indeed all our unproblematised conceits about who and what we are, are unlearnt' (Soudien 2012, 7). I signed up enthusiastically. This represented an opportunity to enrich my own understandings and in particular to develop my approach to teaching around identities, subjectivities and self that are central to the courses I offer in the Women's and Gender Studies Department at UWC.

The course

The course began with a two-day meeting in March 2010 at the University of Stellenbosch, and was followed by online interactions and a final two-day meeting in August. With some trepidation (built around expectations of homework, assignments and evaluation processes) I set off, on the appointed day, to meet my co-learners. A mixed group of about 20 faculty from a range of institutions and disciplines, we were quickly broken up into smaller groups of about 5 or 6. At the risk of reinscribing the very identities my own research as an historian aims to deconstruct, we were men and women, straight and gay, of different classes, ethnicities, languages and generations, and, to employ the apartheid categories that continue to have currency, we were 'white', 'black' and 'coloured'. While we were all privileged to have postgraduate educations and to have careers in academia we were not all positioned in the academy in the same way. Some had decades of teaching experience, others were more junior. Some had doctorates and had published; others were busy with their Ph.D.'s. Some were in relatively senior positions; others were much newer to the academy. While some spoke English as their mother tongue, others had English as a second or even a third language. My anxieties dissipated very quickly. In contrast to several participants, I already had my doctoral degree (from the historically white University of Cape Town). I was also clearly amongst the older and more experienced participants and, furthermore, I already had a modest publishing record. The entire proceedings were conducted in English, my mother tongue, and being what the apartheid regime would have classified as 'white', I was able to draw on the privileges that continue to accrue to 'white' South Africans nearly two decades after the shift to democratic rule. In contrast to my co-learners, key social locations consistently positioned me in advantageous and privileged ways.

I imagined that the participatory methodologies employed, that aimed to alert 'participants to privilege and marginalisation through encounters across difference' (Bozalek 2011, 469), would surface these complex positionalities. We began, for example, with our personal histories, and each asked to use colourful oil pastels to draw the 'river of our lives', drawings which were then used as the basis for reflection. In the next exercise, we used the same pastels to map and then discuss 'our community', and in this way the course moved forward. Differences emerged even before we had begun: where I could hardly wait to get my hands on the crayons, others had felt intimidated. One participant noted in an email on 23 October, 2010, that the drawing exercises 'were quite daunting to me', while another observed in an email on 9 April, 2010, that 'the activities were quite unsettling...drawing with crayons and such, it is not something I'm familiar with anymore, so it was a bit challenging trying to come up with a "good enough" drawing'.

In reflecting on the overall experience once the course had ended members of my group agreed in an email on 5 April, 2010, that there had been a 'very strong feeling of collegiality amongst our group'. Another emailed on 22 April 2010, that the course felt as if she were 'involved in a collaborative workshop with colleagues', while a third commented in an email on 22 April, 2010, that it was 'very refreshing to be with a group of people who were broadly interested in the same stuff'. In contrast, my experiences were less positive. Although, at the start of the course, I had shared the sense of collegiality described by my colleagues I had felt increasingly uncomfortable as it proceeded. As early as mid-morning of the first day, my sense of belonging had given way to frustration and as the course proceeded my irritation and discomfort mounted.

Tensions and frustrations

My irritation lay in the fact that we were a group talking about community largely as a metaphor for race where race seemed to be dislocated from other subjectivities. There was little or no discussion of what it might mean, for instance, that only some of us relished the opportunity to use crayons and colour in class and whether or how this might be linked to a wide range of social locations. Instead, we were talking about race, and talking about race without reference to gender or other positionalities. This was amplified by a reading list where questions around race featured strongly, but where just one (out of about 50 recommended articles) made mention of gender in the title. My frustration grew as it became increasingly clear that understandings of race would not be undergoing a critical analysis of the ways in which race itself is a social construct mediated by other constructs.

I found myself, in other words, a feminist in a space devoted to promoting social justice where gender (let alone other subjectivities) was barely acknowledged – and this in a society in which women have been described as 'under siege' (Gqola 2007, see also Lewis 2009; Ratele 2006; Hassim 2009; Gouws 2005; Steyn and van Zyl 2009; Isike and Uzodike 2011; Salo et al. 2010; Hunter 2011; Bak 2008). I found myself furthermore a feminist historian in a space where the centrality of gender and sexuality to racialised and racist processes of imperialism, colonialism, industrialisation, urbanisation and, more recently, apartheid, were dismissed. I found myself in a space where race was the overarching narrative despite work demonstrating how gender and sexuality, expressed through patriarchal masculinities and heteronormativities, are just as important as race in understanding historical practices of race, of warrior traditions, white supremacy, local liberation movements and patriarchal communities that produce and reproduce the profound social injustices characterising South African society today (see, for example, Scully 1997; van der Spuy 1996; Bradford 1987, 1996; Gevisser and Cameron 1995; Germond and de Gruchy 1997; Achmat 1993; Erlank 2003; Suttner 2009; Unterhalter 2000).

Taking gender (and other positionalities) seriously also means acknowledging that performances of masculinity are deeply harmful to all men, even those occupying locations of privilege. As bel hooks has observed '[p]atriarchy is the single most life threatening social disease assaulting the male body and spirit' (2004, 17; see also Hearn 2007; Woods 2010). In South Africa though, dominant discourses which essentialise gender simultaneously construct gender equity as a zero sum game in which men have nothing to gain and everything to lose. The biological essentialism underpinning the 'inscribed habits of attention' (Dewey in Boler and Zembylas 2003, 127), that weave together the 'everyday fabric of what is considered common sense' (Boler and Zembylas 2003, 111) to unmark gender and sexuality, that narrate the injustices of the past almost entirely around race, have little or nothing to offer men. Such a discourse is deeply problematic for questions of social justice. It is, as Yuval-Davis insists, *precisely* those social divisions that go unmarked or unrecognised that are in fact central, and that to speak about one subject location without reference to another is to risk essentialising both. 'Rendering them visible needs to be an important political project . . . recognition of social power, not of social identities – is of crucial emancipatory importance' for all of us (Yuval-Davis 2006, 201).

Silence, in the face of such theorising, did not seem to be a viable option, particularly when complemented with a feminist understanding of silence as a political act for which we are accountable. Speaking out on the other hand also came at a price. In drawing on the theorising alluded to above, I suggested that it was important we recognise that racialised subjectivities were co-constructed by gender, sexuality and other salient subject positions. My teachers responded by explaining that South Africa's history of racial inequality meant it was both necessary and desirable to concentrate on racial inequalities. I insisted that we risked essentialising race, gender and heteronormativity, unless we acknowledged the ways in which subjectivities mediate and co-construct each other. My teachers explained again that the course was focused on differences structured around race. With this disagreement underpinning interactions over the course of the entire module, I increasingly felt myself positioned as the stereotypical 'white woman who doesn't want to talk about race'. What felt like a negation of both my teaching and my personal belief system produced what could be described as a panic attack, such that by the end of the course, even though all those around me remained gracious, I was, to say the least, deeply discomforted.

Learning through discomfort

In reflecting on the cause and level of irritation, frustration and panic, I experienced I was reminded of the experiences of a colleague almost a decade earlier when he and I were members of a group of 10 feminist academics from the Universities of the Western Cape and the West Indies invited to a Summer Institute at the Women's Studies Department of the University of Maryland, College Park, USA. We spent just over two weeks in often heated discussion and debate with our hosts and colleagues, all bar one of whom were women. The solitary man was Kopano Ratele, a feminist psychologist then based at UWC. He subsequently wrote a paper about the discomforts he experienced at being the only man in the group, and how it felt as if he had 'walked in where one is not supposed to be, akin to crashing an intimate dinner, but somehow the couple goes on being extremely and inexplicably nice, as if they had been expecting you' (Ratele 2001, 77). The paper, in which he drew critical attention to a complex set of emotional attachments expressed as, or through, boundaries of belonging, raises questions about the 'anxieties of belonging' or not belonging, and how we come to not belong, to get 'lost', suddenly struck home (Ratele 2001, 82).

At the Summer Institute it was Ratele's gender, his social positioning (which coincided with self-identification) as 'man', which trumped his sense of self as a feminist academic, and that compromised his sense of feeling at home. In the CSI module, it was my social positioning as 'white', compounded by popular understandings of feminist ideology as a divisive and largely irrelevant Western import (Hassim 2009), that compromised my sense of belonging. For Ratele, belonging meant to conform and he drew attention to how the inevitable disavowal of difference that accompanies conforming meant that '[t]he kind of belonging one wishes for…is one that is permanently suspended, always negotiable' (2001, 82). 'Belonging', in other words, requires concessions, a willingness to give up difference. The difficulty confronting both of us, though, was that even though, like Ratele, I understand race and gender as social constructs, the social positioning they entail is not easily given up.

At the same time, a key component of being 'lost', according to Ratele, lay in being unable to understand, or in misunderstanding, others (Ratele 2001, 78). I wondered about this in relation to my response to feeling 'lost', and the ways in which being unable to make my point heard – that gender and sexuality matter –had compromised my ability to inhabit a feminist identity. Perhaps, in naming my experiences as 'frustration' and 'irritation' I was in fact occupying a location of privilege structured around some or all of the subject locations I identified earlier in this paper. Renaming and reconceiving my responses as 'anxieties' suggested new questions to ask about my engagement with the module, compelling me to think much more carefully about how to understand the overall experience. In locating me in a marginal space and raising questions about the deeply held feminist beliefs informing both my teaching and research, in requiring me to think more carefully about the tensions implicit in Patti Lather's (2001) suggestion that non-mastery is an ethical move, the course certainly elicited the discomfort and careful consideration that provided me with space to reflect and ultimately to a deeper understanding – and stronger commitment – to my feminism. For that, I thank my teachers.

Reflecting on pedagogy

Perhaps, the anxiety and panic I felt during the course were an expected and necessary outcome of the pedagogical approach deliberately employed by the course convenors. They had hoped to explore difference by adopting what Megan Boler and Michalanos Zembylas have termed a 'pedagogy of discomfort' (2003, 129). Such a pedagogy 'urges students as well as educators to move outside of their comfort zones…[and] invites critical inquiry regarding cherished beliefs and assumptions' (Boler and Zembylas 2003, 131). The course certainly achieved that, as evidenced by this paper.

The challenge, however, of teaching for transformation while transforming teaching remains. The difficult times within which South African educators such as myself labour remains characterised by paradox: nothing is resolved. On the one hand, power inequalities shaped by imperialism and colonialism and created in law under apartheid as 'race' have been and remain an important explanatory narrative in South African history. Today many, if not most, South Africans use these categories to self-identify because they have shaped individual lives in meaningful ways and because they continue to serve as both constraints and resources in everyday interactions (Whitehead 2012; Hunter 2011; Seekings 2008; Adhikari 2004). The need, in post-apartheid South Africa, to evaluate change in terms of equity and redress for specific groups further reinscribes the use of race. South African academics (myself included) still use the racialised categories[1] with which we are familiar precisely because they continue to have saliency. As Yuval-Davis observes '[i]n specific historical situations and in relation to specific people' there are 'social divisions that are more important than others in constructing individuals' specific positionings' (2006, 201). To jettison the racial categories with which so many South Africans still identify would represent an elision of profoundly significant experiences of difference, exclusion and struggle.

At the same time however, uncritical deployment of the racial categories invented over centuries of struggle means glossing over the ways in which such identities are always social constructs, always contested, even in their most stable and 'primordial forms' (Yuval-Davis 2006, 199). It is deeply problematic that we continue, as Ratele notes, to 'deploy ~~race~~ as a fact of nature, act as if sex and gender at some moments are un~~raced~~, and almost always completely ignore desire, or at best keep it separate from, the politics of ~~race~~, and similarly sex and gender' (2004, 140, original strikethrough). Perhaps, this helps explain why (in the US at least) students engaged in diversity classes focusing on race and ethnicity are apparently not learning about and from diversity (Barnet 2011, 671). Closer to home, Lange and Singh (2010) have also drawn attention to limitations associated with privileging one aspect of identity in their discussion of the South African educational landscape.

More alarming still is the risk of validating such inventions in contemporary nationalisms (see Robus and Macleod 2006). If we are to heed Paul Zeleza's warning that '[t]he pages of history drip with blood shed by invented identities' (2006, 15), then such nationalisms must be opened to critique. Taking gender, sexuality as well as race and other axes of power and privilege seriously, exploring how they mediate and co-construct each other presents possibilities for understanding the past – and imagining the future – differently. How, for example, might understanding the conflict characterising centuries of South African history as a conflict between racialised versions of heterosexual patriarchal masculinity shape how we teach South African history? How might such teaching shape how our graduates understand social justice and how they might imagine South African citizenship in the future?

It is, as Forrest reminds us, precisely those unmarked categories that need to be surfaced. A key goal of critical pedagogy should be to raise awareness of the structures that hold us back from *within*, to provide space for surfacing complexity and to create space within which teachers and learners are able to challenge their own interpretations of reality (Forrest, Judd, and Davison 2012). The importance of recognising this complexity was underlined by a comment from a gender diverse reader of this paper, a transperson whose embodiment challenges hegemonic understandings of both sex and gender. My experiences of the CSI module reminded him of the 'trauma and emotional exhaustion…[of] a gender reconciliation-breathwork workshop of about 30 people' about 10 years ago. 'For most exercises', he recalled 'women and men were divided into separate groups. I was having to fight all the way to try and undermine the binary discourse – the whole way it reinforced gender stereotypes, heteronormativity, etc'. Eventually he told them, 'well, I don't belong to either of the two groups, so I guess I'll have to make my own group and sit by myself and think about gender diversity. Actually I was kinda ready to bolt.' After making this decision, he was surprised to find a few others wanting to join his group 'because it sounds more interesting'. In the end, this small group included 'individuals from four sex/gender identities (transgender, intersex, female and male), at least three sexual orientations (straight, personality-oriented, asexual), three language groups, three racial backgrounds (black, coloured, white), ages ranging from twenties to sixties and included wheelchair users as well as able-bodied individuals (as noted by ES in a comment on a draft of the paper on 28 July, 2012, see also Morgan, Marais, and Wellbeloved 2009; Morgan and Wieringa 2005).

Conclusion

The difficult times within which South African educators labour, and the more inclusive and transformative education system these times demand, requires more (rather than less) recognition of the social complexity of both the past and the present. Addressing the profound inequalities structured around gender, sexuality and class that co-construct and intersect with race requires the disruption of monolithic and essentialising narratives around race and this needs to permeate our teaching. My undergraduate students have taught me how difficult they find it to see this complexity, how hard they find it to understand gender, sexuality or race as socially constructed expressions of power, of privilege and marginalisation. Despite extensive exposure to gender theorising, interactions with students reveal that even at the end of a course on gender, masculinity can remain largely unmarked (see Clowes 2013). And yet, a future characterised by social justice demands a full understanding of injustice in the past: there is, as Ursula le Guin once said, 'no road, nowhere to go . . . unless the past and the future [are] made part of the present by memory and intention' (Le Guin 1974, 157).

In the last two years, my undergraduate classes have increasingly focused on locations of privilege rather than oppression. I ask my students to explore privilege by drawing on their lived experiences of race, gender, sexuality, class, age, ethnicity, religion (and other subject locations they suggest matter) to consider how they might be privileged and, concomitantly, ways in which their privileges are simultaneously mediated or limited. How, for example, are the patriarchal privileges accruing to male students mediated by race and sexuality? How do race and sexuality intersect with gender to profoundly compromise men's health and well-being, and how do we make sense of this in relation to building a South Africa characterised by social justice? I hope, in 2013, to encourage my students to imagine the kinds of communities they would like to live in in the future, the roles gender, race and other forms of diversity might play (if any?) in these communities, and ways in which they themselves feel constrained or empowered to contribute towards the development of such communities. Perhaps in this I might engage with the call, made over a decade ago by Duncan Brown, for teaching and research that reconciles the demands of difference and national belonging 'not through the fictions of imagined unity, but through a shared problematic' (Brown 2001, 767; Kerner 2012, 211). South African educators need to find ways of talking about a shared future without reinscribing the same 'habits of practice' that constitute the very hegemonic discourses of inequality that require critique. Difficult times indeed for South African educators, but as

Sheldon Kopp (1974, 166) so succinctly observed, while 'you can't get there from here . . . there's no place else to go'.

Acknowledgements

This work is based upon research supported by the National Research Foundation. Thanks to ES, Patricia van der Spuy, Viv Bozalek and Brenda Liebowitz and anonymous reviewers for helpful comments on earlier incarnations of this paper. Thanks also to Anthea Lesch (University of Stellenbosch), Linda Smith (University of the Witwatersrand), Jeff Jawitz (University of Cape Town), Melanie Petersen (University of Stellenbosch) and Sandra Johnson (Cape Peninsula University of Technology) for giving me permission to share some of their experiences of this course.

Note

1. Using inverted commas to signal our discomfort and a footnote to articulate our reservation.

References

Achmat, Z. 1993. "'Apostles of Civilised Vice': 'Immoral Practices' and 'Unnatural Vice' in South African Prisons and Compounds, 1890–1920." *Social Dynamics* 19 (2): 92–110. doi:10.1080/02533959308458553.

Adhikari, M. 2004. "Not Black Enough: Changing Expressions of Coloured Identity in Post-apartheid South Africa." *South African Historical Journal* 51 (1): 167–178. doi:10.1080/02582470409464835.

Bak, M. 2008. "Townships in Transition: Women's Caring Keeps the Township Together." *Journal of Southern African Studies* 34 (2): 255–268. doi:10.1080/03057070802037928.

Barnet, P. E. 2011. "Discussions Across Difference: Addressing the Affective Dimensions of Teaching Diverse Students About Diversity." *Teaching in Higher Education* 16 (6): 669–679. doi:10.1080/13562517.2011.570435.

Boler, M., and M. Zembylas. 2003. "Discomforting Truths: The Emotional Terrain of Understanding Difference." In *Pedagogies of Difference: Rethinking Education for Social Change*, edited by P. Trifonas, 110–136. New York: RoutledgeFalmer.

Bozalek, V. 2009. *Community, Self and Identity: A Cross-institutional Collaborative Teaching and Learning Project Promoting Inclusivity.* http://sanord.uwc.ac.za/usrfiles/users/9174080913/Conference_2009/V_Bozalek.pdf.

Bozalek, V. 2011. "Acknowledging Privilege through Encounters with Difference: Participatory Learning and Action Techniques for Decolonising Methodologies in Southern Contexts." *International Journal of Social Research Methodology* 14 (6): 469–484. doi:10.1080/13645579.2011.611383.

Bradford, H. 1987. "'We Are Now the Men': Women's Beer Protests in the Natal Countryside, 1929." In *Class, Community and Conflict*, edited by B. Bozzoli, 292–323. Johannesburg: Ravan Press.

Bradford, H. 1996. "Women, Gender and Colonialism: Rethinking the History of the British Cape Colony and its Frontier Zones, C. 1806–1870." *Journal of African history* 37 (3): 351–370. doi:10.1017/S0021853700035519.

Brown, D. 2001. "National Belonging and Cultural Difference: South Africa and the Global Imaginary." *Journal of Southern African Studies* 27 (4): 757–769. doi:10.1080/03057070120090727.

Business Day live January 31. 2013. "Regulatory Overkill Threatens Academic Autonomy in South Africa." http://www.bdlive.co.za/opinion/2013/01/31/regulatory-overkill-threatens-academic-autonomy-in-south-africa.

CHE (Council on Higher Education). 2000. *Towards a New Higher Education Landscape: Meeting the Equity, Quality and Social Development Imperatives of South Africa in the 21st*

Century. Pretoria: CHE. http://www.che.ac.za/documents/d000009/New_HE_Landscape.pdf.

Clowes, L. 2013. "The Limits of Discourse: Masculinity as Vulnerability." *Agenda: Empowering Women for Gender Equity* 27 (1): 12–19. doi:10.1080/10130950.2013.778621.

Course Outline. 2010. *Course Outline Community, Self and Identity in Higher Education 2010*. University of the Western Cape & University of Stellenbosch.

Daily Maverick January 31. 2013. "Conversations: Crain Soudien on South Africa's Identity Politics." http://dailymaverick.co.za/article/2013-01-31-conversations-crain-soudien-on-sas-identity-politics.

DHET. 2008. *Report of the Ministerial Committee on Transformation and Social Cohesion and the Elimination of Discrimination in Public Higher Education Institutions*. Pretoria: Department of Higher Education and Training. http://us-cdn.creamermedia.co.za/assets/articles/attachments/21831_racismreport.pdf.

DHET. 2013. *Media Statement: Announcement of the Oversight Committee on the Transformation of South African Universities in Johannesburg*, 24 January 2013. Pretoria: Department of Higher Education and Training.

Draft National Plan for Higher Education in South Africa, Ministry of Education, 2001. http://www.dhet.gov.za/LinkClick.aspx?fileticket=TRydBRRtaTc%3D&tabid=411&mid=1369.

Erlank, N. 2003. "Gender and Masculinity in South African Nationalist Discourse, 1912–1950." *Feminist Studies* 29 (3): 653–671. http://www.jstor.org/discover/10.2307/3178733?uid=3739368&uid=2134&uid=2&uid=70&uid=4&sid=21102616100427.

Forrest, K. A., K. R. Judd, and J. R. Davison. 2012. "Coming to Know Within 'Healthy Uncertainty': An Autoethnography of Engagement and Transformation in Undergraduate Education." *Teaching in Higher Education* 17 (6): 710–721. doi:10.1080/13562517.2012.666733.

Germond, P., and S. de Gruchy. 1997. *Aliens in the Household of God: Homosexuality and Christian Faith in South Africa*. Cape Town: David Philip.

Gevisser, M., and E. Cameron. 1995. *Defiant Desire: Gay and Lesbian Lives in South Africa*. Braamfontein: Ravan Press.

Gouws, A., ed. 2005. *Unthinking Citizenship: Feminist Debates in Contemporary South Africa*. Cape Town: UCT Press.

Gqola, P. 2007. "How the 'Cult of Femininity' and Violent Masculinities Support Endemic Gender based Violence in Contemporary South Africa." *African Identities* 5 (1): 111–124. doi:10.1080/14725840701253894.

Hassim, S. 2009. "Democracy's Shadows: Sexual Rights and Gender Politics in the Rape Trial of Jacob Zuma." *African Studies* 68 (1): 57–77. doi:10.1080/00020180902827431.

Hearn, J. 2007. "The Problems Boys and Men Create, the Problems Boys and Men Experience." In *From Boys to Men: Social Constructions of Masculinity in Contemporary Society*, edited by T. Shefer, K. Ratele, A. Strebel, N. Shabalala, and R. Buikema, 13–33. Cape Town: UCT Press.

hooks, b. 2004. *The Will to Change*. New York: Washington Square Press.

Hunter, M. 2011. "Beneath the 'Zunami': Jacob Zuma and the Gendered Politics of Social Reproduction in South Africa." *Antipode* 43 (4): 1102–1126. doi:10.1111/j.1467-8330.2010.00847.x.

Isike, C., and U. Uzodike. 2011. "Marginalising Women in Politics: Recent Trends in KwaZulu-Natal." *Development Southern Africa* 28 (2): 225–240. doi:10.1080/0376835X.2011.570069.

Jansen, J. 2009. *Knowledge in the Blood: Confronting Race and the Apartheid Past*. Stanford, CA: Stanford University Press.

Kerner, I. 2012. "Questions of Intersectionality: Reflections on the Current Debate in German Gender Studies." *European Journal of Women's Studies* 19 (2): 203–218. doi:10.1177/1350506811434666.

Kopp, S. 1974. *If you Meet the Buddha on the Road, Kill Him!* London: Sheldon Press.

Lange, L., and M. Singh, 2010. "Issues in Quality Assurance in South African Higher Education." In *Equity and Quality Assurance: A Marriage of Two Minds*, edited by M. Martin, 37–73. Paris: UNESCO and International Institute for Educational planning.

Lather, P. 2001. "Postbook: Working the Ruins of Feminist Ethnography." *Signs: A Journal of Women in Culture and Society* 27 (1): 199–227. doi:10.1086/495677.

Le Guin, U. 1974. *The Dispossessed.* St Albans: Granada.

Lewis, D. 2009. "Gendered Spectacle: New Terrains of Struggle in South Africa." In *Body Politics and Women Citizens: African Experiences*, edited by A. Schyler, 125–137. Stockholm: Sida Studies No. 24.

Mail and Guardian Special Report January 28. 2013. *Crisis in Humanities.* http://mg.co.za/specialreport/crisis-in-humanities.

Morgan, R., C. Marais, and J. Wellbeloved. 2009. *Trans: Transgender Life Stories from South Africa.* Johannesburg: Jacana Media.

Morgan, R., and S. Wieringa. 2005. *Tommy Boys, Lesbian Men and Ancestral Wives: Female Same Sex Practices in Africa.* Johannesburg: Jacana Media.

Ratele, K. 2001. "Notes on the Anxieties of Belonging." *Agenda* 50: 77–82. doi:10.1080/10130950.2001.9675996.

Ratele, K. 2004. "Kinky Politics." In *Re-thinking Sexualities in Africa*, edited by S. Arnfred, 139–154. Sweden: Almqvist & Wiksell Tryckeri AB.

Ratele, K. 2006. "Ruling Masculinity and Sexuality." *Feminist Africa* 6: 48–64. http://agi.ac.za/sites/agi.ac.za/files/fa_6_feature_article_4.pdf.

Robus, D., and C. Macleod. 2006. "'White Excellence and Black Failure': The Reproduction of Racialised Higher Education in Everyday Talk." *South African Journal of Psychology* 36 (3): 463–480. doi:10.1177/008124630603600303.

Salo, E., M. Ribas, P. Lopez, and M. Zamboni. 2010. "Living Our Lives on the Edge: Power, Space and Sexual Orientation in Cape Town Townships, South Africa." *Sexuality Research and Social Policy* 7 (4): 298–309. doi:10.1007/s13178-010-0028-8.

Scully, P. 1997. *Liberating the Family: Gender and the British Slave Emancipation in the Rural Western Cape, South Africa, 1823–1853.* Cape Town: David Philip.

Seekings, J. 2008. "The Continuing Salience of Race: Discrimination and Diversity in South Africa." *Journal of Contemporary African Studies* 26 (1): 1–25. doi:10.1080/02589000701782612.

Soudien, C. 2012. *Realising the Dream: Unlearning the Logic of Race in the South African School.* Cape Town: HSRC Press.

Steyn, M., and M. van Zyl. 2009. *The Prize and the Price: Shaping Sexualities in South Africa.* Cape Town: HSRC Press.

Suttner, R. 2009. "The Jacob Zuma Rape Trial: Power and African National Congress (ANC) Masculinities." *Nordic Journal of Feminist and Gender Research* 17 (3): 222–236. doi:10.1080/08038740903117174.

Unterhalter, E. 2000. "The Work of the Nation: Heroic Masculinity in South African Autobiographical Writing of the Anti-apartheid Struggle." *European Journal of Development Research* 12 (2): 157–178. doi:10.1080/09578810008426770.

Van der Spuy, P. 1996. "Making Himself Master: Galant's Rebellion Revisited." *South African Historical Journal* 34 (1): 1–28. doi:10.1080/02582479608671862.

Whitehead, K. 2012. "Racial Categories as Resources and Constraints in Everyday Interactions: Implications for Racialism and Non-racialism in Post-apartheid South Africa." *Ethnic and Racial Studies* 35 (7): 1248–1265. doi:10.1080/01419870.2011.591407.

Woods, J. 2010. "The Black Male Privileges Checklist." In *Privilege: A Reader*, 2nd ed., edited by M. Kimmel and A. Ferber, 27–37. Boulder, CO: Westview Press.

Yuval-Davis, N. 2006. "Belonging and the Politics of Belonging." *Patterns of Prejudice* 40 (3): 197–214. doi:10.1080/00313220600769331.

Zeleza, P. 2006. "The Inventions of African Identities and Languages: The Discursive and Developmental Implications." In *Selected Proceedings of the 36th Annual Conference on African Linguistics*, edited by O. Arasanyin and M. Pemberton, 14–26. Somerville, MA: Cascadilla Proceedings Project. http://www.lingref.com/cpp/acal/36/paper1402.pdf.

Global citizenship, sojourning students and campus communities

David Killick

Centre for Learning & Teaching, Leeds Metropolitan University, Leeds, UK

The paper argues for situating today's students as 'global citizens', emphasising *self-in-the-world* identity over *act-in-the-world* agency. It draws upon a three-year investigation into the lived-experience of sojourning UK undergraduate students, which surfaced examples of significant learning among new communities of practice. Their experiences of crossing learning thresholds is presented as change to the lifeworld, and argued to have enhanced their sense of *self-in-the-world.* Because primary sites of learning identified within the narratives were within inter-subjective encounters outside the host culture and beyond what was planned within their mobility programmes, I suggest that similar learning might be enabled among diverse campus communities at home.

Introduction

> Being alive as human beings means that we are constantly engaged in the pursuit of enterprises of all kinds... As we define these enterprises and engage in their pursuit together, we interact with each other and with the world and we tune our relations with each other and with the world accordingly. In other words we learn. (Wenger 1998)

The work of *tuning our relations with each other* in our daily interactions in a world increasingly enacted amongst alterity becomes ever more complex. Yet our inter-connected world 'screams' for more people who are 'effective in dealing with others in the various dimensions of human interaction' (Lonner and Hayes 2004). It is welcome, therefore, to find university strategic documents aspiring to graduate students as 'global citizens' or similar, and espousing commitments to 'internationalisation'. However, the contested term 'global citizen' is rarely made explicit within these documents, and 'internationalisation' remains for many an income generation exercise. Additionally, in most institutional agendas and the majority of research and best-practice literature, the intersections between internationalisation, equality and diversity, and inclusivity 'at home' are notably absent (for exceptions, see Caruana and Ploner 2010).

The research informing this paper was located in a large UK university in which global citizenship explicitly featured within a five-year cross-university curriculum internationalisation process to integrate *cross-cultural capability* and *global perspectives* (Killick 2006; Jones and Killick 2007). These were argued to represent skills, knowledge-sets and worldviews relevant to the global-citizen-graduate at home or at large. However, I now suggest that such *act-in-the-world* attributes are secondary to an *identification of self* as a member of diverse local and global communities. Such identification, one's sense of *self-in-the-world,* comprises a complex set of affective, behavioural and cognitive schemas, constituting how I stand before myself in the world, as one who recognises as equally human those whose ontologies and sociocultural practices diverge from my own (represented in Figure 1). Locating the development of the self within the boundaries of higher education finds strong echoes in the precepts of significant and transformative learning theories (Rogers 1969; Mezirow 1991; Rogers and Freiberg 1994; Mezirow and Associates 2000), but sits uneasily in discourses of key skills, employability and students-as-customers.

A more globally-situated sense of *self-in-the-world*, though, seems a requirement if our students are to *tune their relations* more easily amongst alterity, and thence bolster their inclination to develop and put to use *act-in-the-world* capabilities. The model of the global citizen underpinning this paper comprises these two dimensions of being – *self-in-the-world* identity and *act-in-the*-world agency; with the first, *'who I am'* taking precedence over the second, '*what I can*'.

Transformative and significant learning – and student mobility

Research into outbound student mobility falls into two camps – that conducted in the context of the 'year abroad' associated with modern languages degrees, principally in the UK, and that conducted in the context of non-compulsory and/or shorter mobility experiences, largely carried out by 'international educators' – until recently, principally in the USA and Australasia, and critiqued by some as being 'blind' to the 'master narrative' driving their practice (Vande Berg 2009). The former, often with a primary focus on developments in linguistic ability, has

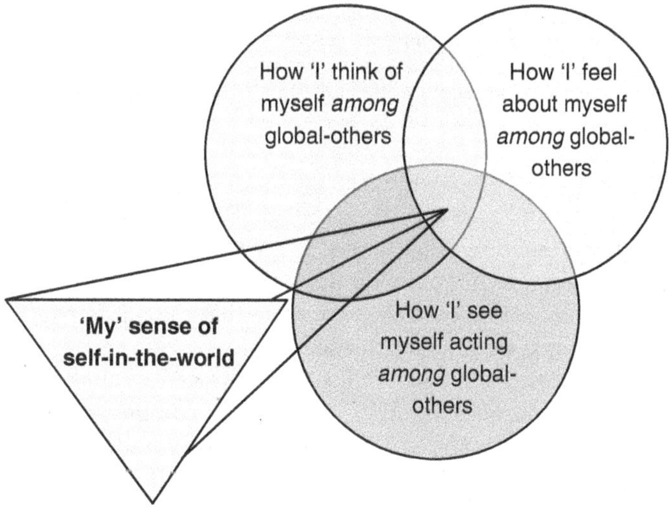

Figure 1. Illustration of the three-dimensional identification of self-in-the-world.

critiqued the transformative nature of the experience (e.g. Coleman 1997, 1999) rather more than the latter, which more consistently reports the 'legion' benefits (Lenz and Wister 2008) of extra-ordinary, transformative learning (for example, various chapters in Savicki 2008a). Both include many small scale studies into how the experience could be improved through preparatory work with the students (and one very extensive project – FDTL 1997–2000), interventions during the mobility (e.g. Vande Berg 2009; Weber-Bosley 2010), post-experience reflection or other activity, and setting up forms of virtual 'exchange' to replace or augment physical mobility (e.g. Ellenwood and Snyders 2010). The study, which underpins this paper included students experiencing both types of mobility, and sought to identify learning commensurate with the development of a sense of *self-in-the-world*. Therefore, although not all research gives positive accounts of outbound mobility outcomes, the brief overview of literature in Table 1 offers examples of some of which do by way of *illustration* (I have conflated/re-named some categorisations, and omitted some less commonly discussed outcomes). Depending upon the specific focus, the research identifies differing sets of new knowledge, skills, and/or attitudes, but the picture is one of students developing personal attributes, such as self-confidence and independence, new-found knowledge about own and/or other culture, more highly developed skills for communicating across cultural boundaries and/or an enhanced interest in international affairs and ways of life.

Many studies in this area are set in the context of intercultural development/ acculturation theory (Bennett 2008), and a few have sought to show the link between the 'life-changing' nature of reported outcomes and the construct of 'perspective transformation' or 'self-actualization' underpinning transformative learning (Mezirow 1991; Mezirow and Associates 2000). Perhaps surprisingly, given that, '[w]hen students talk about study abroad being a life-changing experience, it is the experiential and affective learning that they are talking about' (Savicki 2008b), little consideration appears in the literature on the links between mobility and Rogers'. more holistic account of 'significant learning':

> ...the organized consistent conceptual gestalt composed of perceptions of the characteristics of 'I' or 'me' and the perceptions of the relationships of the 'I' or 'me' to others and to various aspects of life, together with the values attached to these perceptions. (Rogers 1959)

Our model of global citizenship, with primacy upon an evolving sense of *self-in-the-world*, requires such an account of learning. Rogers shares with social and constructivist learning models (Bandura 1977; Vygotsky 1978), the importance of inter-subjective encounter as a/the site for developing our understanding of the world and of ourselves within it. It is in such encounters that the participants in this study found much of their own significant learning.

This paper (1) explores some of the learning surfaced in student narratives, (2) suggests how this encourages a belief that home campus communities might stimulate similar learning for the static student majority and (3) proposes ways in which formal and extended curricula could offer spaces for this to happen.

Table 1. Summary of outcomes identified in selected research 1988–2010.

Study	Self-confidence	Self-awareness/ identity	Maturity/ personal growth	Flexibility & adaptability/ 'open-mindedness'	Independence/ taking responsibility	Patience/ persistence	Empowerment/ individual agency	Empathy & tolerance	Intercultural competencies & communication skills	Awareness of own culture (including multicult-uralism)	Knowledge/ awareness of other culture(s)	A 'global perspective'/ 'world-mindedness'	Global citizenship attributes/ attitudes	Interest in international affairs	Interest in international travel/ volunteering	Foreign language proficiency	Academic attainment	Intellectual 'curiosity'/ interest in learning	Cognitive skills develo-pment	Profe-ssional compe-tencies
1										✓	✓	✓		✓						
2			✓								✓					✓				
3										✓	✓	✓		✓						
4	✓			✓	✓						✓				✓					
5	✓						✓			✓	✓	✓	✓						✓	
6	✓		✓	✓	✓		✓													
7												✓								
8	✓	✓					✓	✓		✓	✓	✓							✓	✓
9				✓		✓		✓	✓	✓	✓						✓			
10	✓	✓					✓			✓	✓	✓								✓
11			✓							✓	✓					✓	✓			✓
12	✓		✓							✓	✓					✓	✓			✓
13	✓									✓	✓			✓						✓
14					✓		✓						✓							
15	✓				✓		✓				✓	✓		✓	✓	✓		✓		
16				✓	✓									✓	✓			✓		
17									✓											
18	✓			✓				✓	✓							✓	✓			
19	✓		✓	✓						✓	✓	✓	✓		✓	✓	✓			✓
20	✓			✓	✓			✓												
21	✓		✓	✓	✓				✓		✓					✓				
22	✓	✓	✓	✓		✓	✓													
23		✓								✓	✓									
24		✓									✓	✓		✓	✓					

Note: (1) Carlson and Widaman (1988); (2) Adelman (1988); (3) Carlson et al. (1990); (4) Thomlinson (1991); (5) Kauffman et al. (1992); (6) Gmelch (1997); (7) Douglas and Jones-Rikkers (2001); (8) Cushner and Mahon (2002); (9) Chieffo and Griffiths (2004); (10) Quezada (2004); (11) Ingraham and Peterson (2004); (12) Sussex Centre for Migration Research and Centre for Applied Population Research (2004); (13) Davis et al. (2005); (14) Fordham (2006); (15) Hadis (2005a); (16) Hadis (2005b); (17) Williams (2005); (18) Stronkhorst (2005); (19) Dwyer (2004); (20) Black and Duhon (2006); (21) Leggott and Stapleford (2007); (22) Chambers and Chambers (2008); (23) Janes (2008); and (24) de Grosbois, Kaethler, and Young (2010).

The background research

Over a three-year study, the lived-experiences of undergraduate students participating in different international mobility experiences in Europe and Australia were explored in depth. Participants were from a range of disciplines, and their mobility experiences contributed differently to their study programmes. Having purposefully sampled the range of activity types, participants were selected by convenience. The purposeful sampling was based upon variables within the design parameters of the mobility itself, or within the participants' own accommodation choices (summarised in Table 2). The objective of this approach was to allow the exploration of lived-experience not to be constrained by specifics *within* a single mobility type. To ensure anonymity, all participants have female pseudonyms.

I interviewed participants prior to departure, travelled to shadow them and interview them *in situ*, and interviewed again 6–12 weeks post-experience. Around 213,000 words were transcribed for analysis. The exploration of the data adopted a phenomenological approach to develop rich individual descriptions of participants' lived-experiences. These were used for more interpretative manoeuvres (the phenomenological 'imaginative variation' [see, for example, Moustakas 1994]) to develop structural descriptions, drawn upon below.

Learning spaces

A rich finding concerns how more globally-situated senses of *self-in-the-world* emerged within newly-established communities of social practice (cf. Wenger 1998). I have described elsewhere (Killick 2012b) how two types of 'special relationships' (with specific 'significant others', or through membership of international communities) emerged as particularly rich sites of learning. Other forms of social encounter and community were also noted by individual participants. Tiff and Clare found a community of 'affect' (Szerszynski and Urry 2002) among fellow sporting enthusiasts; Rita, Joan, Gill, and Clare variously established friendships among local or international housemates; professional communities among their peers were particularly important to Rita, Anne and Deborah. Their narratives came alive with accounts of brushing against the lifeworlds of 'countless amounts of people, and from all the different places' (Gill), 'mixing more with different people from different cultures...cultures and communities' (Lisa), and 'making friends with different cultures...and nationalities' (Tiff). Significantly for this paper, with only a few exceptions, these relationships emerged outside the principal mobility community, and were entirely 'serendipitous' – not planned into the mobility experience by either the organisers or the participants. These were the spaces in which learning thresholds were crossed and virtuous learning circles occurred.

Thresholds and circles

We can represent the acquisition of a threshold concept (Meyer and Land 2005; Meyer, Land, and Baillie 2010) as a (re)formulation of an aspect of the lifeworld, through which significant further learning becomes possible (and without which this learning is unlikely to be possible). Within inter-subjective encounters, participants variously experienced threshold-crossing relevant to their envisionings of themselves

Table 2. Mobility variables considered at the sampling stage.

	Anne	Deborah	Belinda	Tanya	Rita	Paula	Joan	Margaret	Christine	Clare	Lisa	Betty	Gill	Tiff
	France		Romania		Spain				Australia					
Volunteering			✓	✓										
Working	✓	✓			✓	✓								
Studying							✓	✓	✓	✓	✓	✓	✓	✓
Duration (weeks)	4	4	2	2	30	30	30	30	15	15	15	15	15	15
Realistic to travel home in mobility					✓	✓	✓	✓						
Foreign language users	✓	✓			✓	✓	✓	✓						
Credit-bearing & directly assessed	✓	✓							✓	✓	✓	✓	✓	✓
Credit-bearing & not directly assessed					✓	✓	✓	✓						
Self-funded (whole or part)			✓	✓					✓	✓	✓	✓	✓	✓
Found individual accommodation					✓					✓			✓	
Shared 'international' accommodation						✓	✓	✓	✓					✓
Shared peer accommodation	✓	✓	✓	✓							✓	✓		

and others, and of their approaches to future encounters. We may represent this as a significant move in which dimly visible cultural others cross lifeworld horizons to stand as more hued and familiar individuals. Such a move represents grasping a powerful threshold concept, through which it becomes more feasible for other vague and/or potentially inhospitable lifeworld representations of distant lands, cultural practices and apparently alien values to be opened and explored, precisely because they have assumed a human dimension. The individual phenomenological descriptions reveal a range of examples:

> For Belinda: Gypsy communities in general have become less distant, and their world more complex than she'd imagined. Poverty, previously a theoretical phenomenon, imposed itself into her lifeworld as visceral, personalised, and much closer to home.
>
> For Lisa: New intimates with names and histories carried with them new cultures, and through coming to know these individuals she became more tolerant and more curious. In particular, she developed a sense of Chinese, Vietnamese and Malaysians as discrete, personalised, nationalities.
>
> For Tiff: From encounters here, other cultures now stand closer, met, interacted with, personalised; these reinforced her general ethics of openness and tolerance.
>
> For Rita: The local population raised her awareness of cultural differences, enabling her to see a place populated by individuals who stood beyond her stereotypes. The extended-worlds of Spain, South American and European cultures more generally became more personalised to her.
>
> For Joan: The overt, welcoming friendships of her international social group enabled her to draw once slightly threatening distant places into her lifeworld. As the extended-worlds of 'other cultures' took more personalised form, South America, Italy and France have become places to be explored.

A second threshold concept in the narratives is the etic perspective that a participant's culture stands differently in the lifeworlds of others. Through such realisation the potential to broaden other perspectives on self, culture and nation emerges. Belinda recognised how she might not be seen by the local Gypsy community as the benevolent volunteer of her own envisioning, standing instead in the shadow of previous visitors:

> [They] don't necessarily know where we're from and what we're doing . . . and . . . they've had people before coming in, and taking photographs, and raising money for themselves . . . so it's that lack of trust.

Betty became more 'sort of conscious of . . . who you are' in the world. Aware of:

- herself as outsider:

> . . . we're trying to come into their life. We're going to go back to England and they're . . . they're going to have to stay here, and that's . . . this is their life;

- how she might 'come across to other people', leading her to 'question myself and the way that I am around other people'; and

- how British university life (which she continues to see 'as quite normal and as quite healthy') might appear to others: 'I think it's odd for them'.

Based upon a new awareness of how her own cultural rituals appear to others, Rita was able to critique her own responses and change her behaviour:

> ...in Spain everybody says, 'I want.' And for me that seems really rude. If I go into a restaurant I would never, ever, in England, dream of saying, 'I want this.' But in Spain you had to adapt to it, because if you start by, 'Oh well, if it doesn't bother you, please could I have...,' [...] They're just going to walk away thinking you've not decided.

This represents a further threshold concept – the realisation that communication with cultural others requires noticing, or mindfulness (Langer 1989), as part of *taking responsibility for one's own role in an interaction.*

We see in these brief examples how participants found affective, behavioural and cognitive triggers and thresholds pushing lifeworld change. In Rita's single narrative, we see how the three dimensions of learning interacted in a holistic development cycle (she *felt* uncomfortable *experiencing* behaviours which are rude in her own culture, she *reflected* upon that in the context of her current situation, and now *behaves* differently). For Tanya, *thinking* about 'their stories' changed her *feelings* towards the Gypsy community, and she emphasised the power of shared communal *experience*: 'We've eaten here. We've drunk here – you know...'

The narratives surface other examples of learning crossing dimensions, and of how such development goes with participants in new senses of self as 'one who has' and therefore 'can again' cross cultural boundaries; setting up a virtuous circle of new becoming. Clare found confidence through the experience of having witnessed herself interacting with cultural and social others, '[I've] made my way with so many new people who you wouldn't meet in any normal times', 'why would there be anything to fear' in any similar situation back in the future? Gill, buoyed by many successful intercultural interactions returned home confident that: '...where other people are from or who they are doesn't stop me from talking to them, not being afraid of people or anything.'

Bringing it all back home

I have presented examples of significant learning surfaced through the narratives of undergraduates on international mobility experiences. Thresholds were crossed through:

- personalising the once distant 'other'
- perceiving *that* others envision one's own cultural practices differently
- recognising own cultural rituals as arbitrary and potentially offensive to others
- witnessing oneself in successful interaction with cultural others

I am not proposing that the participants' lifeworld shifts have transformed them into global citizens, but we may see that they have begun to 'develop habits of coexistence: conversation in its older meaning, of living together, association' (Appiah 2006, xix), and in such 'habits' is self-identity forged. Since these students experienced this learning within inter-subjective encounters most frequently with sociocultural others, who were *outside* the host community or the planned mobility activities, can our campuses, rich with diversity spanning nationalities, ethnicities, languages, genders, ages, socioeconomic class, and the rest, offer spaces in which *all* students are enabled to personalise the others they encounter, experience habits of coexistence and cross similar learning thresholds?

Gill reported that:

> I'd say that I don't ignore people from other cultures... back at home... I guess what I'm trying to say is that,... I don't come across people from other cultures in Leeds – but when the situation arises I will talk to them and I will help them out..., but <u>here</u> [in Australia] it's kind of hard <u>not</u> to get involved with people from other countries, because it's... all the international students together....

We have to ask, how, on a Gill's campus, with over 100 nationalities of student, a swathe of ethnicities and religions, which prides itself on its achievements in widening participation, is it possible to not 'come across people from other cultures'? What several participants evidenced is that through intercultural inter-subjective encounters they came (in some measure at least) to identify themselves as an *international*, as a member of a community, which extends beyond established sociocultural boundaries, in ways which they clearly had not in England. (How) can we facilitate successful intercultural encounters on our home campuses to stimulate threshold crossing and a sense of *self-in-the-world* which is commensurate with global citizenship? While the dominant discourse revolves around skills, employability and/or 'customers', this may seem far removed from the role and purpose of higher education. However, the joy which the participants evidenced in their personal growth suggests that students might find re-envisioning their university journeys inspirational – as might many in the academic community. This leads us to consider what in much of Europe has been referred to as *internationalisation at home* (Crowther et al. 2000; Beelen 2007) as part of a *comprehensive internationalisation* (Hudzik 2011) agenda. Space does not allow any detailed exploration of this model of internationalisation, but I conclude with three key developments to our practice, which I suggest would go some way to establishing a campus culture/environment in which all students might find transformative border crossing more feasible.

Embedding cross-cultural capability within the formal curriculum

While developments in modern languages education argue for a focus on the understanding of self in relation to the intercultural other (Byram and Zarate 1997; Phipps and Gonzalez 2004; Crawshaw 2005; Alred, Byram, and Fleming 2006), such is not the case in most disciplines. Many colleagues would argue that such matters have no bearing on their subject area. However, most if not all of our students will enact their disciplinary expertise (and their daily lives) in contexts where they need to 'interact with each other and with the world'. Constructive alignment theory (Biggs 2003, 2007) directs us towards learning outcomes as the driver for both assessment and the design and delivery of associated learning experiences. Leaving aside the degree to which a constructivist learning paradigm is compatible with the prescription of learning outcomes, embedding aspects of cross-cultural capability *within* subject learning outcomes has the potential to drive our practice to enhance student awareness of, and capabilities for successful intercultural interactions. By way of a single, simple example, (see, for further examples, the case study in Jones and Killick 2013) many modules have a learning outcome along the lines of:

> Students will be able to make a presentation analysing [xyz]

This might be modified to locate the original subject requirements in a more global and multicultural world:

> Students will be able to make a presentation analysing [xyz] which is accessible to an audience of native and non-native speakers of English

That students are capable of such mindfulness and adjustments was clear among the research participants who moved with increasing freedom within their international student communities.

Structuring equitable course-based student interactions

In Allport's much cited *contact hypothesis*, key conditions for 'successful' intercultural meetings (i.e. meetings which might *reduce* prejudice across the participants) include 'equal status contact between majority and minority groups', 'the pursuit of common goals', 'reaching below the surface', 'contact that leads people to do things together', and activity which is condoned by 'authority' (Allport [1954] 1979). The first four of these, at least, characterised contacts within the participants' emerging communities discussed above. Can we say the same of the ways in which encounters on our courses are currently structured or enacted? Among the limited research in this area, student narratives have shown the equality requirement to be lacking with regard to levels of language ability and the types of knowledge privileged within the interaction space (Ippolito 2007), and while care must be taken not to promote a stereotypical or deficit model of 'the' international student, numerous articles identify potential cultural differences in epistemologies, and approaches to study and academic authority, which arguably impact upon the equity of our learning spaces and activities. Bache and Hayton (2012) present an interesting picture of how such differences might manifest themselves with respect to aspects of inquiry-based learning, for example. This is not to argue for a radical overhaul of our practice, but to suggest that mindfulness regarding the potential for inequities within the intercultural student encounters created within our courses might serve all students well in advancing a more global sense of self.

Encouraging students to cross sociocultural boundaries beyond the formal curriculum

How are new students 'inducted' into their university (how common is it to hold *separate* international student welcome events, for example)? What emphasis, if any, is placed upon multicultural interactions, inclusive behaviours, international encounters by the university, student residencies or the Students' Union? Notwithstanding several decades of concern about the isolating experience of international students coming to study on campuses in the UK, Australasia and North America, successful large scale interventions to engender integrated campus communities seem rare, and often responsibilities for crossing cultural boundaries are seen to lie with the international student rather than with the dominant local group. Concerns about this recently led the UK Council for International Student Affairs and the Higher Education Academy to commission a number projects to research and enhance mechanisms for linking home and international students on UK campuses (HEA/ UKCISA 2012). At the time of writing, the dissemination event for these projects has not occurred, but one set of staff and student-facing resources have been released through a creative commons licence (Killick 2012a, 2012c).

Summary

We have the ingredients to situate university life as a dwelling among alterity for everybody, but we need to re-envision the university community. Institutionally, we are perhaps guilty of imagining that bringing diversity onto campus will, in and of itself, generate border crossings and inclusive communities of practice. At course and module level, we are perhaps guilty of forgetting that creating equitable learning spaces is part of our responsibilities as educators. This is not to gainsay either the efforts of individual tutors to internationalise their curricula, often with great invention and impact (e.g. Strauss, U, and Young 2011). Rather, it is to suggest that if these remain isolated and happenstance events in a student's journey through university experienced only in isolated pockets of the formal curriculum (Leask 2009), their impact is unlikely to be transformative. Like all of us, and perhaps all the more so as they struggle towards self-authorship (Baxter Magolda 2001, 2009), our undergraduate students will be drawn by the ease and comforts of communities of similitude. McTighe et al. (1999) refer to college campuses as 'the multivalent space bringing people from all kinds of backgrounds into potential relationship with one another' (cited in Barnett 2011). Experience suggests that engaging in such relationships remains more potential than realised; not surprising if such 'ambivalent and conflicted' encounters, characterised as 'act[s] of vulnerability' (Barnett 2011) are left to chance within an environment which privileges the dominant local, and in so doing legitimises their own ghettoisation.

The participants who informed the background research in this article were *drawn or driven* to engage with the diversity they encountered as they embarked upon an adventure in a bigger world, almost regardless of the formal design features of their various mobility experiences. When each of our students set forth on the adventure of their university education, they are also at a point of embarkation. The institution and the discipline they encounter need to be experienced as spaces in which inclusive participation across whatever sociocultural boundaries might present themselves is the expectation, the requirement and *the norm*. How we design the curriculum, learning activities and assessments, and the pervading institutional ethos to shape our students' encounters with their peers has the potential to enable or to disable threshold crossings and the formulation of a more globally situated sense of *self-in-the-world.* Such a sense, may well enhance their employability, facilitate the development and deployment of important key skills and even improve their satisfaction as customers. More fundamentally, their *higher* education will have helped them make their way in their world.

References

Adelman, M. B. 1988. *The Impact of an International Education on College Acceptance and Career Development, American Institute for Foreign Study.* ERIC Document Reproduction Service No. ED 298 056.

Allport, G. [1954] 1979. *The Nature of Prejudice.* Cambridge, MA: Perseus Books.

Alred, G., M. Byram, and M. Fleming, eds. 2006. *Education for Intercultural Citizenship: Concepts and Comparisons.* Edited by M. Byram and A. Phipps. Vol. 13, *Languages for Intercultural Communication and Education.* Clevedon: Multilingual Matters.

Appiah, K. A. 2006. *Cosmopolitanism: Ethics in a World of Strangers.* New York: Norton.

Bache, I., and R. Hayton. 2012. "Teaching in Higher Education." *Inquiry-based Learning and the International Student* 17 (4): 411–423. doi:10.1080/13562517.2011.641003.

Bandura, A. 1977. *Social Learning Theory.* Englewood Cliffs, NJ: Prentice-Hall.

Barnett, P. E. 2011. "Discussions Across Difference: Addressing the Affective Dimensions of Teaching Diverse Students About Diversity." *Teaching in Higher Education* 16 (6): 669–679. doi:10.1080/13562517.2011.570435.

Baxter Magolda, M. 2001. *Making Their Own Way: Narratives for Transforming Higher Education to Promote Self-development.* Sterling, VA: Stylus.

Baxter Magolda, M. 2009. "Educating Students for Self-Authorship: Learning Partnerships to Achieve Complex Outcomes." In *The University and its Disciplines. Teaching and Learning Within and Beyond Disciplinary Boundaries*, edited by C. Kreber, 143–156. London: Routledge.

Beelen, J., ed. 2007. *Implementing Internationalisation at Home.* EAIE Professional Development Series for International Educators. Amsterdam: European Association for International Education (EAIE).

Bennett, M. J. 2008. "On Becoming a Global Soul." In *Developing Intercultural Competence and Transformation: A Path to Engagement during Study Abroad*, edited by V. Savicki, 13–31. Sterling, VA: Stylus.

Biggs, J. 2003. "Aligning Teaching and Assessing to Course Objectives." Presented at the Teaching and Learning in Higher Education: New Trends and Innovations Conference, University of Aveiro, April 13–17.

Biggs, J. 2007. *Teaching for Quality Learning at University: What the Student Does.* Maidenhead: SRHE & Open University.

Black, H. T., and D. L. Duhon 2006. "Assessing the Impact of Business Study Abroad Programs on Cultural Awareness and Personal Development." *Journal of Education for Business* 81 (3): 140–144. doi:10.3200/JOEB.81.3.140-144.

Byram, M., and G. Zarate. 1997. *Definitions, Objectives and Assessment of Socio-cultural Objectives.* Strasbourg: Council of Europe.

Carlson, J. S., B. B. Burn, J. Useem, and D. Yachimowicz. 1990. *Study Abroad: The Experience of American Undergraduates in Western Europe and in the United States.* Westport, CT: Greenwood Press.

Carlson, J. S., and K. F. Widaman. 1988. "The Effects of Study Abroad During College on Attitudes Toward other Cultures." *International Journal of Intercultural Relations* 12 (1): 1–18. doi:10.1016/0147-1767(88)90003-X.

Caruana, V., and J. Ploner. 2010. *Internationalisation and Equality and Diversity: Merging Identities, A Case Study of Policy and Practice at Six Universities.* London: Equality Challenge Unit.

Chambers, A., and K. Chambers. 2008. "Tuscan Dreams. Study Abroad Student Expectation and Experience in Siena." In *Developing Intercultural Competence and Transformation: Theory, Research and Application in International Education*, edited by V. Savicki, 128–153. Sterling, VA: Stylus.

Chieffo, L., and L. Griffiths. 2004. "Large-scale Assessment of Student Attitudes after a Short-term Study Abroad Program." *Frontiers: The Interdisciplinary Journal of Study Abroad* X: 165–177.

Coleman, J. A. 1997. "Residence Abroad within Language Study." *Language Teaching* 30 (1): 1–20. doi:10.1017/S0261444800012659.

Coleman, J. A. 1999. "Language Learner Attitudes and Student Residence Abroad: New Qualitative and Qualitative Insights." In *Poetics and Praxis of Language and Intercultural*

Communication, edited by D. Killick, M. Parry, and A. Phipps, 75–95. Leeds: Leeds Metropolitan University, Glasgow University Press.

Crawshaw, R. 2005 "Intercultural Awareness as a Component of HE Modern Language Courses in the UK." *Subject Centre for Languages, Linguistics and Area Studies Good Practice Guide.* Accessed September, 2013. http://www.llas.ac.uk/resources/gpg/2303.

Crowther, P., M. Joris, M. Otten, B. Nilsson, H. Teekens, and B. Wächter. 2000. *Internationalisation at Home: A Position Paper.* Amsterdam: European Association for International Education.

Cushner, K., and J. Mahon. 2002. "Overseas Student Teaching: Affecting Personal, Professional, and Global Competencies in an Age of Globalization." *Journal of Studies in International Education* 6 (1): 44–58. doi:10.1177/102831530200600l004.

Davis, I., M. Evans, P. Cunningham, G. Fredriksson, G. Pike, H.-F. Rathenow, A. Sears, F. Tesch, and P. Whitty. 2005. "Developing Citizenship through International Exchanges." In *Citizenship and Higher Education: The Role of Universities in Communities and Society*, edited by J. Arthur, 134–157. Abingdon: RoutledgeFalmer.

de Grosbois, D., J. Kaethler, and A. Young. 2010. "Discovering the World – Discovering Myself." In *Internationalisation and the Student Voice*, edited by E. Jones, 68–82. London: Routledge.

Douglas, C., and C. G. Jones-Rikkers. 2001. "Study Abroad Programs and American Student Worldmindedness: An Empirical Analysis." *Journal of Teaching in International Business* 13 (1): 55–66. doi:10.1300/J066v13n01_04.

Dwyer, M. M. 2004. "More Is Better: The Impact of Study Abroad Program Duration." *Frontiers: The Interdisciplinary Journal of Study Abroad* X: 151–163.

Ellenwood, A. E., and F. J. A. Snyders. 2010. "Virtual Journey Coupled with Face-To-Face Exchange: Enhancing the Cultural Sensitivity and Competence of Graduate Students." *Intercultural Education* 21 (6): 549–566. doi:10.1080/14675986.2010.533036.

FDTL. 1997–2000. *Learning and Residence Abroad Project*. Accessed September, 2013. https://www.llas.ac.uk//lara/programme.html.

Fordham, T. 2006. "Pedagogies of Cultural Change: The Rotary International Youth Exchange Program and Narratives of Travel and Transformation." *Journal of Tourism and Cultural Change* 3 (3): 143–159. doi:10.1080/14766820608668492.

Gmelch, G. 1997. "Crossing Cultures: Student Travel and Personal Development." *International Journal of Intercultural Relations* 21 (4): 475–490. doi:10.1016/S0147-1767(97)00021-7.

Hadis, B. F. 2005a. "Gauging the Impact of Study Abroad: How to Overcome the Limitations of a Single-cell Design." *Assessment & Evaluation in Higher Education* 30 (1): 3–19. doi:10.1080/0260293042003243869.

Hadis, B. F. 2005b. "Why Are They Better Students When They Come Back? Determinants of Academic Focusing Gains in the Study Abroad Experience." *Frontiers: The Interdisciplinary Journal of Study Abroad* XI: 57–70.

HEA/UKCISA. 2012. *HEA and UKCISA Open Internationalisation Funding Call.* http://www.heacademy.ac.uk/projects/detail/internationalisation/connections/Connections_Pilot_Projects.

Hudzik, J. 2011. *Comprehensive Internationalization: From Concept to Action.* New York: NAFSA. http://www.nafsa.org/Resource_Library_Assets/Publications_Library/Comprehensive_Internationalization__From_Concept_to_Action/.

Ingraham, E. C., and D. L. Peterson. 2004. "Assessing the Impact of Study Abroad on Student Learning at Michigan State University." *Frontiers: The Interdisciplinary Journal of Study Abroad* X: 83–100.

Ippolito, K. 2007. "Promoting Intercultural Learning in a Multicultural University: Ideals and Realities." *Teaching in Higher Education* 12 (5–6): 749–763. doi:10.1080/13562510701596356.

Janes, D. 2008. "Beyond the Tourist Gaze?: Cultural Learning on an American 'Semester Abroad' Programme in London." *Journal of Research in International Education* 7 (1): 21–35. doi:10.1177/1475240907086886.

Jones, E., and D. Killick. 2007. "Internationalisation of the Curriculum." In *Internationalising Higher Education*, edited by E. Jones and S. Brown, 109–119. London: Routledge.

Jones, E., and D. Killick. 2013. "Graduate Attributes and the Internationalised Curriculum: Embedding a Global Outlook in Disciplinary Learning Outcomes." *Journal of Studies in International Education* 17 (2): 165–182. doi:10.1177/1028315312473655.

Kauffman, N. L., J. N. Martin, H. D. Weaver, and J. Weaver. 1992. *Students Abroad, Strangers at Home: Education for a Global Society.* Yarmouth, ME: Intercultural Press.

Killick, D. 2006. *Cross-cultural Capability & Global Perspectives. Guidelines for Curriculum Review.* Leeds: Leeds Metropolitan University. http://repository.leedsmet.ac.uk/main/view_record.php?identifier=8134&SearchGroup=Open+Educational+Resources.

Killick, D. 2012a. *Connections – Developing a Global Outlook Bringing Together Diverse Students through the Learning Experience (staff resource).* Leeds: Leeds Metropolitan University. Accessed December, 2012. http://repository.leedsmet.ac.uk/main/view_record.php?identifier=6965&SearchGroup=Open+Educational+Resources.

Killick, D. 2012b. "Seeing-Ourselves-in-the-World: Developing Global Citizenship Through International Mobility and Campus Community." *Journal of Studies in International Education* 16 (4): 372–389. doi:10.1177/1028315311431893.

Killick, D. 2012c. *Student Connections.* http://studentconnectionsstage.ntistudio.ac.uk.

Langer, E. 1989. *Mindfulness.* Reading, MA: Addison-Wesley.

Leask, B. 2009. "Using Formal and Informal Curricula to Improve Interactions Between Home and International Students." *Journal of Studies in International Education* 13 (2): 205–221. doi:10.1177/1028315308329786.

Leggott, D., and J. Stapleford. 2007. "Internationalisation and Employability." In *Internationalising Higher Education*, edited by E. Jones and S. Brown, 120–134. London: Routledge.

Lenz, W., and J. Wister. 2008. "Short-term Abroad with Long-term Benefits." *International Educator.* 84–87.

Lonner, W., and S. Hayes. 2004. "Understanding the Cognitive and Social Aspects of Intercultural Competence." In *Culture and Competence, Contexts of Life Success*, edited by R. Sternberg and E. Grigorenko, 89–110. Washington, DC: American Psychological Association.

McArthur, J. 2010. "Achieving Social Justice within and through Higher Education: The Challenge for Critical Pedagogy." *Teaching in Higher Education* 15 (5): 493–504. doi:10.1080/13562517.2010.491906.

McTighe, M. C., M. Garcia, C. A. Hudgins, M. T. Nettles, W. E. Sedlacek, and D. G. Smith, eds. 1999. *To Form a More Perfect Union: Campus Diversity Initiatives.* Washington, DC: Association of American Colleges and Universities.

Meyer, J. H. F., and R. Land. 2005. "Threshold Concepts and Troublesome Knowledge (2): Epistemological Considerations and a Conceptual Framework for Teaching and Learning." *Higher Education* 49 (3): 373–388. doi:10.1007/s10734-004-6779-5.

Meyer, J., R. Land, and C. Baillie, eds. 2010. *Threshold Concepts and Transformational Learning*. Boston, MA: Sense.

Mezirow, J. 1991. *Transformative Dimensions of Adult Learning*. San Francisco, CA: Jossey-Bass.

Mezirow, J., and Associates, eds. 2000. *Learning as Transformation: Critical Perspectives on a Theory in Progress.* San Francisco, CA: Jossey-Bass.

Moustakas, C. E. 1994. *Phenomenological Research Methods.* Thousand Oaks, CA: Sage.

Phipps, A., and M. Gonzalez. 2004. *Modern Languages: Learning and Teaching in an Intercultural Field.* London: Sage.

Quezada, R. L. 2004. "Beyond Educational Tourism: Lessons Learned while Student Teaching Abroad." *International Education Journal* 5 (4): 458–465. http://www.iejcomparative.org/data/volumes/v5n4.pdf.

Rogers, C. R. 1959. "A Theory of Therapy, Personality and Interpersonal Relationships as Developed in the Client-centered Framework." In *Psychology: A Study of a Science. Vol. 3: Formulations of the Person and the Social Context*, edited by S. Koch, 184–256. New York: McGraw-Hill.

Rogers, C. R. 1969. *Freedom to Learn: A View of What Education Might Become.* Columbus, OH: Charles E. Merrill.

Rogers, C. R., and H. J. Freiberg. 1994. *Freedom to Learn.* New York: Merrill.

Savicki, V., ed. 2008a. *Developing Intercultural Competence and Transformation: Theory, Research and Application in International Education*. Sterling, VA: Stylus.

Savicki, V. 2008b. "Experiential and Affective Education for International Educators." In *Developing Intercultural Competence and Transformation: Theory, Research and Application in International Education*, edited by V. Savicki. 74–107. Sterling, VA: Stylus.

Strauss, P., A. U, and S. Young. 2011. "I Know the Type of People I Work Well With: Student Anxiety in Multicultural Group Projects." *Studies in Higher Education* 36 (7): 815–829. doi:10.1080/03075079.2010.488720.

Stronkhorst, R. 2005. "Learning Outcomes of International Mobility at Two Dutch Institutions of Higher Education." *Journal of Studies in International Education* 9 (4): 292–315.

Sussex Centre for Migration Research and Centre for Applied Population Research. 2004. *International Student Mobility*. Brighton and Dundee: HEFCE, SHEFC, HEFCW, DEL, DfES, UK Socrates Erasmus Council, HEURO, BUTEX, British Council.

Szerszynski, B., and J. Urry. 2002. "Cultures of Cosmopolitanism." *The Sociological Review* 50 (4): 461–481. doi:10.1111/1467-954X.00394.

Thomlinson, T. D. 1991. *Effects of a Study Abroad Program on University Students: Toward a Predictive Theory of Intercultural Contact*. ERIC Document Reproduction Service No. ED332629.

Vande Berg, M. 2009. "Intervening in Student Learning Abroad: A Research-based Inquiry." *International Education* 20 (4): S15–S27. doi:10.1080/14675980903370821.

Vygotsky, L. S. 1978. *Mind in Society: The Development of Higher Psychological Processes*. Cambridge, MA: Harvard University Press.

Weber-Bosley, G. 2010. "Beyond Immersion. Global Engagement and Transformation Through Intervention via Student Reflection in Study Abroad." In *Internationalisation and the Student Voice*, edited by E. Jones, 55–67. London: Routledge.

Wenger, E. 1998. *Communities of Practice: Meaning, and Identity*. Cambridge, MA: Cambridge University Press.

Williams, T. R. 2005. "Exploring the Impact of Study Abroad on Students' Intercultural Communication Skills: Adaptability and Sensitivity." *Journal of Studies in International Education* 9 (4): 356–371. doi:10.1177/1028315305277681.

Strategies for critiquing global citizenry: undergraduate research as a possible vehicle

Juliet Henderson

Department of History, Philosophy and Religion, Oxford Brookes University, Oxford, UK

Even as an increasing number of universities commit to producing graduates possessing the attributes of 'a global citizen', discussions between academics suggest it is common practice to design programme outcomes which include the attribute of global citizenship without advancing discussion as to ways of embedding them in deeper learning. This presents a potential risk of defaulting to 'empty rhetoric' when trying to meet institutional agendas relating to graduate attributes. To address this issue, this paper opens up discussion about how to assess global citizenship within and across disciplines by offering an example of a four-step method. To support a further goal of framing global citizenship in contemporary Higher Education Institutions as an object of pedagogic and social theory, emergent findings of a discourse of interculturality in student work are presented. Findings serve to identify the ways in which students articulate the contested concept of interculturality, a key attribute of the 'global citizen'.

Introduction

This paper is motivated by the question: 'How can we invite undergraduates to contextualise new global citizenship knowledge and identity in assessment?' I argue for the use of ethnographic-style research as a strategy for going beyond tick-box approaches to graduate attributes, which also promotes the generation of student-authored new knowledge emerging from undergraduate research. For the purposes of this paper, I provide examples of such knowledge in two excerpts from a Dutch student's essay that reveal ways in which she articulates a personal reading and writing of global citizenship knowledge identity, which conforms to the conventions of academic rhetoric and yet offers resistance to individualised and reified readings of 'the global citizen'. This article does not offer a comprehensive textual analysis of undergraduate global citizenship knowledge in the genre of the research essay, rather it uses a discourse-historical interpretation of traces of interculturality in a student text to highlight how critical global citizenship is contextualised at the local level of text, course and institution. It is intended that a more in-depth discourse-historical analysis of student articulations of an English-language discourse of interculturality will be presented in a future paper. Although the locus of analysis for this paper is a course in intercultural communication in the discipline of applied linguistics, it is intended that there are resonances with other practices in other disciplinary traditions.

In this paper, I first argue that the knowledges developed in Byram's set of competencies identifying 'the intercultural speaker' (2009) are fit for the social purposes and processes of educating critical (global) citizens (Guilherme 2002). Next, I contextualise the course and assignment in relation to pedagogical principles and aims before offering a four-step model that can be applied in different disciplines. I then theorise student essay writing as part of the social process of education, which requires students to engage with the textually mobile concepts of self and other, and make choices about what is included or suppressed in their writing. Finally, I interpret two excerpts from a student essay to consider how adequate their use of language is as instances of preference for a critical vision of the non-neutral term of global citizen over a normative vision.

Opening the door to interculturality in the university

The current context of an increased diversity in higher education arguably creates conditions, which are apt for the fostering of graduates who will be responsible, ethical citizens and conciliators in globalised contexts. As an ideal type, such graduates correspond to Byram's notion of 'the intercultural speaker' (2009), or 'intercultural citizen' (2006), who seeks actively to understand both how he or she comes to 'know' others, and the evidence that determines that knowledge (Jordan LLAS 2002). In this sense, the intercultural speaker can be characterised as, in a state of constant evolution between the interrelated processes of gaining intellectual knowledge about difference, and gaining experiential knowledge about difference through discussion and dialogue. Both of these learning processes are conceptualised as reducing stereotyping, prejudice and misunderstanding through the widening of social horizons. In neither case is knowledge considered as an element of the world existing independently from the macro and micro contexts of language, society, and interaction. Indeed, context is seen as an intuitive and effective device for explaining how the interrelated workings of knowledge, language and action produce our social worlds.

Central to all such knowing is the idea that cultural and social life is mediated through language. As 'intercultural speakers', we alternate constantly between individual and social perspectives on knowledge, language and action, which produce mid-level patterns of meaning that allow us to construct experience as meaningful in some ways and not in others (Gee 2005). Byram categorises the five epistemological stances towards the knowledge needed to be interculturally competent under the umbrella term of one of the two French equivalents of the English verb 'to know': *savoir*. Specific to the meaning of *savoir* is the notion of knowledge as a form of social practice. *Savoir comprendre* entails the learning of how to interpret and relate familiar and unfamiliar texts and signs. *Savoir apprendre/faire* identifies skills of 'knowing how to know', and skills of interacting to gain new knowledge or discovering new knowledge. *Savoirs*, or 'knowing' refers to knowledge of self and other acquired through interaction, both between individuals and between self and society. *Savoir être* refers to attitudes involved in relativising the self and valuing the other. *Savoir s'engager* is an important later addition to the framework meaning literally 'knowing how to commit oneself' through the development of political and critical awareness. Since it is intrinsic to the rationale for this course that all students should learn how to engage with sensitive moral and social issues, and develop a questioning attitude towards normative values, Byram's categories of interculturality strongly inform the way knowledge is conceptualised within its teaching and learning approaches, including the assessment design and marking criteria.

It should be pointed out that within universities, such intercultural knowing can be acquired naturally in a variety of contexts, including the library, the coffee bar, and an interaction between tutor and student (Turner 2011). However, frequently little is done by tutors to allow students to become critically aware of this rich resource, and equally little is done by students to engage with such 'close otherness' (Čok 2006). It would seem then that something must be done to engage students in the liberating experience of stepping outside their comfort zones.

The educators, the issues, and the course

In today's increasingly corporate and 'promotional' university (Fairclough 1993), there is an ongoing relevance to the unpacking of everyday social interaction practices, since such practices are important drivers of change. Indeed, each interaction contains the opportunities either to increase or reduce inequality and power differences (Jadhav 2011), and either to sidestep or embrace the human challenge of mediating self understanding through the encounter with other(s). As intercultural educators, we cannot be neutral concerning such opportunities (Freire 1998). Instead, we work actively to prevent the subverting and trivialisation of education in the name of corporate horizons. Our praxis as educators is premised on principles of openness in learning and teaching that is grounded in the ethics of personal development and personal responsibility that we try to translate into 'real practice in the classroom' (McArthur 2010, 499). More specifically, we see this as requiring transparency in the teaching of the ideologies we are using to 'hail' our students as subject global citizens: a critical alternative ideology. In the context of this course and its assignment, this translates into a central aim of extending students critical and experiential understanding of how their understanding of their own identity, or 'self', is necessarily defined through the difference with 'other'.

It is not easy for most undergraduates to step outside of their pre-conceived and often insular understanding of who they are (Lutz 2010, 716). Even though they may have spent a gap year abroad or travelled regularly, many have never acquired the tools for examining their own cultural identity from a critical 'outsider' perspective. Our challenge as educators is twofold. First, a meaningful and reflective encounter between self and other must be organised. Second, to scaffold this learning process, an appropriate set of assessment criteria and assessment design are required. The important point here is that both the assignment design and criteria serve as a 'thinking device' (Gee 2005) that allows students to problematise and question their understanding of identity from a decentred position. In other words, from a position which makes it possible for students to challenge the preconceptions they bring to their accounts of the nature of cultural identity and see it afresh (Hammersley 1992, 33). More specifically, such a position should allow students to become concretely aware of the struggles involved in the negotiation of a legitimate student identity as promoted by different groups (Hammersley 1992, 33) and as instanced in the local context of an interview with peers, and the wider context of the university. It is just such a position we relate to the graduate attribute of 'an awareness of own culture and perspective'.

Method for course design

The four-step method for course design (Henderson 2013, 8) is here conceptualised as follows:

1. Break down the assessment criteria to include knowledges and skills apt to foster critical (global) citizens using, for example, Byram's five *savoirs*
2. Open up the assessment design to include the student voice (student as producer not consumer)
3. Clearly scaffold the different parts of the written assignment
4. Map out the research process for gaining new knowledge about self and other

In the course, students are introduced to two main models of cultural identity that theorise it as: (1) an inherited resource, which we play with creatively and dynamically in different contexts (Holliday, Hyde, and Kullman 2004); and (2) as the culturally indexed manner of managing interpersonal relations, or 'rapport', through language use (Spencer-Oatey 2000). These two models are chosen to clearly establish connections between micro relations of language in context and macro relations of social inquiry (Pennycook 2001, 5). In other words, they serve to guide students in their conceptualisation of the ways that their conversations in the university context are legitimated by the wider social context, and vice versa.

The main assessment requires students to conduct ethnographic style interviews with colleagues to collect data apt to inform a response to the research essay title: 'Seeing Me, Seeing you: An investigation into students' cultural identity and intercultural engagement in a twenty-first century Higher Education context'. Both task instructions and assessment criteria are openly conceptualised as a form of soft technology for producing interculturality.

The question is, how do students translate scrutiny of the self and other, which plays a central part in the interview and its transcription and coding, into the constraints of the discursive moves of academic writing? Furthermore, how do they build a bridge between individual knowledge and understanding of interculturality to social knowledge and understanding, as structured in the genre of an academic essay with clear guidelines for its division into sections?

The remainder of this paper focuses on an interpretation of two excerpts from a student essay produced in response to the task outlined above. A brief problematising of the critical discourse analytical approach used to guide the textual interpretation is given in the next section, before moving on to answering the question: 'How does an undergraduate contextualise new global citizenship knowledge and identity in a written assessment?'

Arguing interculturality in the genre of an academic essay

In previous sections, the contextualised relationships between institution, genre convention, individual language use and action have been implicitly and explicitly conceptualised as the dialectically-related drivers of intercultural knowledge production. From a discourse analysis perspective, such associations between ways of thinking, evaluating and talking about for example, interculturality, are developed over time and become naturalised as 'discourses' that are repeated over different times and contexts (Gee 2005). Each individual will relate to and articulate such discourses in different ways in different genres of text, and when doing so will be influenced by competing discourses. For example, there is a clear tension between the normative global citizen as construed in corporate statements of texts of the World Economic Forum, and the normative global citizen as encoded in more radical representations of the global citizen.

Seen 'critically', such textual representations are characteristic of hegemonic uses of power, which aim to naturalise common-sense understandings of what is normal and so secure power through consent and closure (Gramsci 1988): hence they are frequently politically inflected. Texts then become ideologically invested in the manner by which they aim to influence and control the social world (Fairclough 2001). As such, they can be conceptualised as sites of ideological struggle over different ways of reading and representing the world. Fairclough (2003) argues ideology can be uncovered in texts by determining whether a claim has causal effects intended to reproduce or change normative power relations. However, regardless of the individual's perception of the ethical rightness and integrity of these diverging discourses of global citizenship, including their ideological dimensions, it is precisely such hybridity, with different storylines and situated meanings, which advances an enduring knowledge of global citizenship, and causes resonances in our everyday and specialised language use over space and contexts.

What keeps the supra-dynamics of such discourses going is 'power', conceptualised by Foucault as something invisible 'which circulates' (1980, 98), and though it is 'never located here or there' (Foucault 1980), nevertheless serves to constrain and subjectify individuals within different systems of governance. Thus, 'individuals are the vehicles of power, not its point of application' (Foucault 1980); they are its 'carriers' (Gee 2005). Whilst Foucault's model is too metaphysical to support analysis of power in context (Pennycook 2001), it serves to complement the notion of the interculturally *speaking* subject with the notion of the interculturally *spoken* subject. Following this line of thought, we arrive at a dynamic model of the undergraduate subject caught between (1) the dialectical tensions of being simultaneously author of global citizenship knowledge texts and authored by global citizenship knowledge texts, and (2) subject to the 'webs of significance' of university regimes of rational academic rhetoric, conventionally and generically enacted in an essay. By outlining such dialectics, we wish to de-emphasise an overly top-down causality and manipulation of intercultural knowledge, and also to acknowledge the challenge created by students being required to articulate their own subjective views on self and other, using the rhetorical objectivity and stance of neutrality required by the inscription of scientific rationality embodied in the genre of the undergraduate essay. It is with this awareness of the complexity and institutional expectations surrounding the production and reception of social knowledge, that we proceed to an account of argument in academic discourse and a critical approach to its discourse analysis relevant to our exploration of how undergraduates situate themselves as 'carriers' of interculturality within the rhetorical regularisation of the essay (Bazerman 1988).

Argumentation shapes in academic rhetoric, habitually defined according to the western assumption of linear logic (Turner 2011, 92), are adopted to align with reader expectations of 'consistency of gaze [that enables] a steady walk through the argumentation' (Turner 2011.). These shapes are what legitimate claims to producing valid knowledge in the majority of academic genres and contexts. In such traditions of argumentation, the linear trail of logic begins with the main premise that serves to locate the argument within disciplinary borders and map out the area of knowledge to be investigated. For the student whose essay serves as data in this paper, the premise that interculturality is an emergent property of dialogue across difference and positively contributes to diversity in the context of the UK twenty-first century university is implicitly identified in the essay title given. The task of making it explicit is that of the student. Within argumentation theory, the overview function of the main premise is developed and underpinned by *topoi*, which are the parts of argumentation that either explicitly or implicitly establish a relationship between evidence and the claim (Reisigl and Wodak 2001, 74–75), and thus serve as signposts leading the reader from premise to conclusion.

Central to the expectations surrounding the undergraduate argument as a genre is the *sina qua non* that *topoi* are justified using not just the dynamic intertwinings of individual language use and opinions, but also by referencing and critically engaging with the 'other' of authors in the field, seen as key custodians of the discipline and its historical evolution. From a slightly different perspective, the inter-relational dynamics of self and other implicit within the argumentative strategies adopted to achieve the particular aim of passing the course, or excellent performance in the course, can be traced to its anticipated audience, the course tutor, who not only constrains the arguments made through the framing devices of task brief and assessment criteria, but also evaluates how well students have trod the fine line between being subjective and objective (Andrews 1995), all the finer in ethnographic argument and writing. In this sense, the student author, who is both subject and agent of the argument is the one responsible for proving the premise to be 'true', and that this is so on the basis of information obtained through certain interactions of their own 'self' with three categories of 'other' that serve as required elements in the discursive production of interculturality. In the case of this course, these interactions can be mapped out schematically as a linear sequence:

1. Reading of authors in the field to map out perspectives on knowledge that determine the *topoi* of their own research and arguments
2. Face-to-face interaction with fellow interviewees, accompanied by recording and followed by note-taking
3. Reflexive interpretation and identifying of patterns in relations between self and other using the resource of their transcribed encounters
4. Comments on validity of interpretative coding and transcription from fellow interviewees
5. Feedback on the first draft of the essay from the course tutor

It is through their use of the resources of language to mediate and articulate these conversations with others that students build their lines of reasoning arguing the link between the particular of personal experience and observation in context, and the wider knowledge domain of interculturality, *ergo* writing their position as global citizens.

When set against the complexity of the textually mobile concepts of self and other that students must contend with, if there is to be certain robustness to their claims and warrants, it can be seen that knowledge of interculturality is not attained lightly. In order to represent an understanding of the topic, students must learn, grasp, question and infer from knowledge about identity and communication located in a range of constrained but open textual, structural and lexical alternatives. This bears witness to the fact that although acquiring one of the categories of knowledge linked to the graduate attribute of global citizenship involves rhetorical conventions, these are anything but 'empty'. Rather, this process of using language to produce ethical global citizen knowledge, located in meaningful mid-level patterns is what Gee calls 'really effective knowledge' (2005, 66) of 'the human being' (Barnett 2004), since it is used to let the individual go about the social practices of communicating and acting as a global citizen, without having to consciously think about it all the time.

Argument analysis of two traces of a discourse of interculturality in an undergraduate essay

In keeping with the scope of this paper the analysis undertaken focuses on two of the *topoi* articulated in the essay of a Dutch female student. The two *topoi* have been chosen as representative language use embodying the tensions between the interculturally *speaking* subject and the interculturally *spoken* subject. In each case, I am interested in the ways she uses her 'bottom-up' student voice to challenge common-sense understandings of the global and local intercultural context from within the conventions of academic rhetoric.

When examining the language of argumentative strategies used to construe complex and diverse meanings of interculturality in an academic essay, I use the discourse, historical approach, outlined by Reisigl and Wodak (2001, 45). This approach affirms that there is no ontological distinction between microcontext and macrocontext on the other, since 'text production equals system production' (Weiss and Wodak 2003, 4). As a critical discourse analysis method it was first devised to study the discursive strategies used to construct national identity (Wodak et al. 2009), and in this paper, it is contended that there are similarities between this and other forms of collective imaginary and identity, including the discursive construal of global/intercultural identity. Given that the relationship between these strategies is argument-internal, they are distinct but not discrete. There are four strategies for constructing discursive representation that need to be identified to reveal ideological systems and representations (Reisigl and Wodak 2001, 45). These are:

1. *Referential/nomination strategies* used to construe and represent wider social contexts;
2. *Predicational strategies* used to give more or less positive characteristics to social actors;
3. *Perspectivation* the way speakers express their involvement in for example, the academic discourse of interculturality, and position their point of view in its reporting;
4. *Intensification and mitigation strategies* the way the epistemic status of propositions are intensified or mitigated.

My analysis of these is limited; however, I argue that these examples reveal the linguistic inscription of dynamic epistemological assumptions about global citizenship knowledge, in such a way as to suggest a real effect on individual beliefs, ideological positions and identity.

Representing globalisation as inevitable or not

In student A's essay introduction which, according to the assignment brief scaffolding of the different sections of the essay, should 'frame the issues arising from the everyday diversity and plurality in HE, in today's globalized world', the following *topos of globalisation as an engine of change* is identified:

> The world is becoming more globalized, the relationship between cultures, economies and technologies are rapidly intertwining (Doyle and Smith 2002). The effects of globalization are not only experienced in a worldly perspective, even on a local level the consequences are noticeable. Universities see an influx of international students . . .of which a rising number came from outside the European Union'.

Referential strategies

Of interest in the first sentence is the effect produced by sentence level differentiation between (1) 'the world' and (2) globalisation as a process. Rather than subsuming 'the world' into the irresistible and hegemonic processes of the nominalised form of 'globalisation', the student places 'the world' in the main topic position at the beginning of the sentence. This aspect of sentence-level patterning of meaning serves four functions. First, it uses the syntactic resources of the sentence to represent 'the world' as a social actor that is changing in certain ways. Second, it figures the world as the wider context in which changing relations between cultures, economies and technologies are occurring. Third, by representing the world as positioned in a two-way relationship with the processes of globalisation, it ties the representation of the world to logic consistent with the openness to change and difference that is fundamental to the epistemological tenets of interculturality. Lastly, it validates the student's identity as an intercultural speaker through use of content and function words (Gee 2005), which articulate certain ways of thinking and knowing, and through reference to authoritative others within the field of academic knowledge.

Predicational strategies and perspectivisation

No positive or negative characteristics as such are given to the reconfiguring of society as a global and local society produced by the processes of globalisation. Instead, a neutral and technical register is privileged when portraying shifts in relationships between the three pillars of today's social world: cultures, economies, and technology. Such objectivity as a way of wording the world is conventional within the domain of academic knowledge inquiry and representation. Student A's preference for this register here imbues her language with the status of an authoritative representation of the wider context, which disavows subjective figuring of the world. In this way, she presents herself as a detached observer of the globalising world. She defines it as a process. She knows how globalisation processes impact on a local context. Yet she does not represent herself in the language used.

Intensification and mitigation strategies

Concerning the status of the effects of globalisation as *an engine of change*, there is an intensification of positive, or in this case dynamic attributes supporting this claim:

- the adverb 'rapidly' and the present participle form 'intertwining' that follows it, together form a metaphor portraying the speed at which new relationships between cultures, technologies and economies are being made, and hence nation-state boundaries being blurred
- the word 'even' serves to record surprise at the force of the effects of globalisation, since this is significant enough to lead to change straddling different contexts
- the use of the liquid metaphor 'an influx' portrays the experience of the shores of one culture being no longer impenetrable to infiltration by unfamiliar meanings and 'international student' identities (Wu 2001, 125). Here, the metaphor serves to legitimate the opening of borders to new and different identities that positively inflect the local context with transnational dimensions. Such use of metaphor indicates a small shift between different styles of meaning making; from the purely objective to the creative.

All of the above serve to sharpen the illocutionary force of the assertion that the effects of globalisation are producing significant change across contexts. The use of metaphor as an intensification strategy also allows the student to present herself/himself as a creative observer of the globalising world. She/he can categorise it according to taxonomy different to the objective abstractions of academic argument. She/he can use metaphor to define its effects. She/he can interpret globalisation subjectively using her/his imagination.

These two and a half sentences from Student A's introduction can be seen as a snapshot of student use of language to construe an authoritative representation of relations between the 'everyday' and the 'globalized world', which accords with the social languages (Gee 2005) of the academy. By looking at one *topoi* alonc from the argumentative strategies deployed by Student A, it is possible to identify a range of text-internal discursive strategies for legitimating notions of plurality and so resisting notions of essentialism for framing the wider context, or the closed inevitability of globalisation. From a text-external perspective, such strategies also serve the reflexive purpose of reflecting the way the world is 'out there' whilst constructing, or reproducing, a local globalised context.

Personalising engagement with the discovery of new knowledge

In the second section in student A's essay which, according to the assignment brief scaffolding of the different sections of the essay, should be a brief research method section, in which the use of an ethnographic interview approach is justified, whilst recognising its limitations, the *topos of legitimacy of ethnography as a research method* is (not surprisingly) identified. This is traced in the two excerpts from this section below, the first of which directly references the authoritative voice of 'others' in the literature, and the second of which is a textual enactment of the reflexive self:

1. An ethnography is a complex research method for collecting valuable data which provides perspective on a certain topic, in this case cultural differences in a higher education context (Blommaert and Jie 2010).
2. the insights were fascinating, recognisable and easily linked to specific theories

Referential strategies

Reference to the position of ethnography includes terminology which explicitly and implicitly evaluates the positive traits of ethnography as a tool for knowing and detailing the specific ethos, and multiple perspectives of cultural communities. Indeed, the linguistic term 'ethnography' serves metonymically to represent social practices of plurality and openness. By relativising the referentiality of ethnography, the social logic of heterogeneity is textured into the main line of reasoning. In terms of causal powers, 'ethnography' is presented as the subject of a declarative clause with high epistemic status. Though negative attributions can be used to denote ethnographic methods – 'contextual assessment norms can be skewed' – by articulating such limitations in the text, the author does the academic rhetoric equivalent of a *volte-face,* since to acknowledge negative traits of a research project within the text usually serves to eliminate critique from the outside, and so strengthen an argument concerning its validity as a knowledge collecting and interpreting instrument.

Predicational strategies and perspectivisation

The adjective 'complex' is used to qualify the noun ethnographic 'research method'. In the context of the sentence, the connotation of 'complex' is positive, since it yields 'valuable data'. This value relates to an economy of difference, in which the voices of others and their perspective on a topic serve to enrich personal and public knowledge; in this case, about the higher education context. The sentence implies a valuable/less valuable comparison between data, which remains open to uncertainty and complexity, and data which is closed and gives easy, ready answers. By introducing ethnography in this way, the student presents herself/himself as a researcher committed to the difficulty inherent in inferring knowledge from *thick description.* There is a clear avowal that she/he can only know partially and from a situated perspective.

Intensification and mitigation strategies

In the statement by student A, 'the insights were fascinating, recognisable and easily linked to specific theories', intensification of the personal value of conducting research into the situated nature of cultural identity is linguistically realised through a juxtaposed series of characteristics. These begin with two adjectives, which legitimate the task as a process of discovery, which are then connected to a dependent clause using the conjunction 'and'. This latter clause serves to legitimate the interest of the task from a personal perspective through its resonance with voices of authoritative 'others'. The mutual implication of these two parts of the statement is that the research provides findings, which are intelligible from the perspective of personal and academic knowledge.

We can read this *topos* as clear engagement with ethnography as a tool of discovering and producing knowledge. Though it is inherently difficult to use, such difficulties are backgrounded in overall argumentative strategies, which show its individual and collective potential.

Conclusion

In this paper, I have explored the pedagogical positions and practices apt to make it possible for students to challenge the preconceptions they bring to their accounts of intercultural identity, and so develop as 'intercultural' and 'global' citizens. The outcomes of these practices have then been tested against traces of interculturality as contextualised in admittedly circumscribed excerpts from an essay. In this conclusion, I will summarise the overall findings, and in doing so comment upon how critical discourse analysis of argumentative strategies helps open up discussion about the ways in which students resist deeper mainstream ideologies of the value of individual cultural identity in today's increasingly corporate university.

Looking first at the influence of the 'thinking device' of the course content and assessment design on student identity, as embodied in the discursive strategies and linguistic devices used by one student in their essay to build an argument, or storyline, clear evidence of their role as a 'carrier' of interculturality has been identified. Both the *topoi* discussed discredit homogenous notions of singular cultural identity by using different argumentative strategies for representing the university context inter alia as heterogeneous and complex. The student uses differing modalities, sentence structures, metaphors and word choices to convey values, beliefs and ideological positions. These serve to build positive representation in the eyes of the reader/tutor, and have her/him persuaded by the student's legitimacy as interculturality 'carrier'. The second *topoi* also gives positive characteristics to ethnography as a tool which generates knowings aligned with Byram's *savoir comprendre, savoir apprendre/faire, savoirs*, and *savoir être*. Evidence of *savoir s'engager* can be found in a certain commitment to questioning of normative values, albeit within the constraints of the essay genre. As has been noted, though this genre convention favours a rhetorical objectivity, formal register discourse markers and a stance of neutrality in 'its acting out of social structure' (Halliday 1978, 2), this does not preclude use of certain features of language to represent aspects of the world from a different, more subjective perspective. However, in accomplishing their purpose of persuading the reader of their interculturality, this student does not choose to use linguistic means differing significantly from the conventions stipulated by the UK higher education community. What is problematic in this point, and indeed all of the summarising of the findings, is that only two excerpts from one essay are considered.

Future studies will hopefully look in more detail at mainstream and alternative textual instantiations of 'the global citizen' as a graduate attribute, whose use as a signifier is increasing in different social, economic and cultural contexts.

References

Andrews, R. 1995. *Teaching and Learning Argument.* London: Cassell.

Barnett, R. 2004. "Learning for an Unknown Future." *Higher Education Research and Development* 23 (3): 247–260. doi:10.1080/0729436042000235382.

Bazerman, C. 1988. *Shaping Written Knowledge.* Madison: The University of Wisconsin Press.

Blommaert, J., and D. Jie. 2010. *Ethnographic Fieldwork: A Beginner's Guide.* Bristol: Multilingual Matters.

Byram, M. 2006. "From Intercultural Communicative Competence to 'Intercultural Citizenship' – Reflections on the raison d'être of Foreign Language Teaching." In *The Close Otherness*, edited by L. Čok, 21–36. Koper: Založba Annales.

Byram, M. 2009. "Intercultural Competence in Foreign Language Education." In *The Sage Handbook of Intercultural Competence*, edited by D. Deardoff, 321–332. Thousand Oaks, CA: Sage.

Čok, L., ed. 2006. *The Close Otherness.* Koper: Založba Annales.

Fairclough, N. 1993. "Critical Discourse Analysis and the Marketisation of Public Discourse: The Universities." *Discourse and Society* 4 (2): 133–168. doi:10.1177/0957926593004002002.

Fairclough, N. 2001. *Language and Power.* 2nd ed. Harlow: Longman.

Fairclough, N. 2003. *Analysing Discourse: Textual Analysis for Social Research.* London: Routledge.

Foucault, M. 1980. *Power/Knowledge: Selected Interviews and Other Writings 1972–1977.* Brighton: Harvester.

Freire, P. 1998. *Pedagogy of Freedom: Ethics, Democracy, and Civic Courage.* Lanham, MD: Rowman & Littlefield.

Gee, J. P. 2005. *An Introduction to Discourse Analysis; Theory and Method.* 2nd ed. New York: Routledge.

Gramsci, A. 1988. *Prison Letters.* Translated and introduced by Hamish Henderson. London: Zwan in association with the Edinburgh Review.

Guilherme, M. 2002. *Critical Citizens for an Intercultural World.* Clevedon: Multilingual Matters.

Halliday, M. A. K. 1978. *Language as Social Semiotic.* London: Edward Arnold.

Hammersley, M. 1992. *What's Wrong with Ethnography? Methodological Explorations.* London: Routledge.

Henderson, J. 2013. *Teaching Global Citizenship: A Case Study in Applied Linguistics.* York: Higher Education Academy. http://www.heacademy.ac.uk/resources/detail/disciplines/english/global_citizenship.

Holliday, A., M. Hyde, and J. Kullman. 2004. *Intercultural Communication: An Advanced Resources Book.* London: Routledge.

Jadhav, S. 2011. "Global Citizenship as a Graduate Attribute: Cultures of Teaching and Global Well Being." Paper presented at the ESRC seminar series, University College London, December 16.

Jordan, S. 2002. *Intercultural Issues in Foreign Language Learning and Ethnographic Approaches to Study Abroad.* York: Centre for Languages, Linguistics and Areas Studies. http://www.llas.ac.uk/resources/gpg/100.

Lutz, J. 2010. "Becoming Global Citizens without Leaving Home." *Teaching in Higher Education* 15 (6): 715–720. doi:10.1080/13562517.2010.522085.

McArthur, J. 2010. "Achieving Social Justice Within and Through Higher Education: The Challenge for Critical Pedagogy." *Teaching in Higher Education* 15 (5): 493–504. doi:10.1080/13562517.2010.491906.

Pennycook, A. 2001. *Critical Applied Linguistics: A Critical Introduction.* Mahwah, NJ: Lawrence Erlbaum.

Reisigl, M., and R. Wodak. 2001. *Discourse and Discrimination: Rhetorics of Racism and Antisemitism.* London: Routledge.

Spencer-Oatey, H. ed. 2000. *Culturally Speaking.* New York: Continuum.

Turner, J. 2011. *Language in the Academy: Cultural Reflexivity and Intercultural Dynamics.* Bristol: Multilingual Matters.

Weiss, G., and R. Wodak. 2003. *Critical Discourse Analysis: Theory and Interdisciplinarity.* Basingstoke, Hampshire, New York: Palgrave Macmillan.

Wodak, R., R. de Cillia, M. Reisigl, and K. Liebhart. 2009. *The Discursive Construction of National Identity.* 2nd ed. Edinburgh: Edinburgh University Press.

Wu, K.-M. 2001. *On Metaphoring: A Cultural Hermeneutic.* Leiden: Brill.

Interdisciplinary content, contestations of knowledge and informational transparency in engineering curriculum

Sarah Barnard, Tarek Hassan, Andrew Dainty and Barbara Bagilhole

School of Civil and Building Engineering, Loughborough University, Loughborough, UK; Department of Social Sciences, Loughborough University, Loughborough, UK

With the introduction of key information sets (KIS) for all university programmes in the UK from 2012, the character, content and delivery of university degrees may be increasingly used by potential students to differentiate between degree programmes. Therefore, developments in curricula and the relationship to the profession are of growing importance. In this paper, we explore the role of programme content in prospective students' decision-making and describe the prevalence of interdisciplinary content in civil engineering curricula. Following this, we detail student perceptions of interdisciplinary content. It is found that universities currently operate a varied approach to transparency regarding curriculum; students pay little attention to programme content before embarking on their chosen degree; and engineering students view interdisciplinary content in the curriculum with ambivalence, usually ascribing its necessity in the preparation for post-university employment.

Introduction

Current debates around the nature of academic boundaries and movements towards more interdisciplinary education in universities open up interesting avenues for investigations: not only in the academic and professional practice of disciplines, but in how these practices inform curriculum and impact on students themselves. With the planned compulsory introduction of key information sets (KIS) for all university programmes in the UK from 2012, the character, content and delivery of university degrees may be increasingly used by potential students to differentiate between degree programmes. KIS have been developed by the Higher Education Funding Council for England (HEFCE) in order to allow prospective students to access comparable information on full-time or part-time courses (HEFCE 2012a), which is argued to enable students to make an informed choice about where and what to study (BBC 2011). Universities are expected to collect and publish on their websites fifteen pieces of information ranging from student views on quality of the course, resources, feedback, salary and destination of graduates, tuition fees, accommodation costs, 'contact' hours per week and assessment methods. KIS represents a continuation of an emphasis on higher education (HE) performance indicators that can be used to hold institutions accountable for their performance, to inform budgetary allocations and assist in the targeting of policy initiatives, to inform student choices via institutional comparison and to support institutional self-publicity (Pugh, Coates, and Adnett 2005, 21, see also HEFCE 2012b). Originally, HEFCE performance indicators focused on the informational needs of government, policy-makers and the institutions themselves (Pugh, Coates, and Adnett 2005, 25), but now we can see a shift in emphasis towards providing information in relation to decisions about what and where to study. The concept of 'informed choice' is characterised by the development of multiple sources of information for prospective students, of which KIS represents but one. These include careers guidance in schools, university data publication, league tables, teaching quality audits, and the national student survey (NSS), Destinations of Leavers from Higher Education (DLHE survey), web portals (DirectGov and UNISTATs) and also what may be termed 'private sector brokerage' (Davies 2012).

Arguments for the development of information aimed at prospective students emphasise the impact that informed choice will make on enhancing quality in HE. In this discourse it is assumed that it is possible to observe performance, that visibility leads to transparency and that this then leads to improvement (Strathern 2000). The possibility that transparency is different and may be at odds with enhancing quality is highlighted by Strathern (2000). Strathern (2000), utilising Tsoukas's (1997) work on the proliferation of audits and league tables, suggests that transparency of information is artificial and may actually conceal more than it reveals. Reasons for this include problems with performance indicators themselves (Strathern 2000, 314): for example DLHE data, which informs part of KIS, has important data missing, small sample sizes and no control groups (Davies 2012). In addition, indicators that students view as important, for example – earnings after graduation – may be an inappropriate guide to earnings much later (Davies 2012). This and other elements that appear in KIS are argued to be misleading and flawed; 'it does not appear that data on graduate salaries or student satisfaction can, in the majority of cases, provide students with a reliable basis for choice between alternative courses' (Davies 2012, 272). Clearly, there are issues around the validity and philosophical basis for increasing information that is aimed at prospective students.

This paper explores the availability of information for prospective students in HE, developments in curriculum and the relationship to the professions via an examination of a single academic discipline – civil engineering. An historical overview of civil engineering in UK HE describes the particularities of the discipline and how its relationship with the profession has evolved. Following this, we explore student perceptions of interdisciplinary content to develop an understanding of how the civil engineering discipline is interpreted and negotiated, and how innovations in content are experienced and perceived by students over the course of their study. This will enable a more nuanced understanding of how trends towards interdisciplinarity in HE and the profession impact on students themselves.

Civil engineering – evolution of a discipline

In the early days of the UK engineering profession, skills and knowledge were acquired through an apprenticeship: the fundamentals of mathematical, scientific and design principles were learned 'on the job', and there was scepticism about the development of formal education. Even Brunel expressed caution with regard to theoretical training, which was a typical attitude during the early nineteenth century (Buchanan 1989). However, during the industrial revolution, influences from France underlined the need to train engineers more fully in scientific principles (Gregory 1971). The Institution of Civil Engineers, founded in 1818, disseminated technical information and acted as the main network within the profession.

Early engineering education focused upon theoretical scientific principles that underpinned the more applied design approach students would apply in practice. Given that they would gain qualified status only once meeting the requirements of professional institutions, it was these that 'controlled professional practice and the entrance to it' (Gregory 1971, 151). Formal engineering education consisted of pockets of activity in universities as there was a more general reluctance to embrace a substantial move towards a wide-scale education to replace the practical, work-based learning already established in the profession. It was concern about the nation's ability in the technical fields in comparison to those overseas – a response to the Paris Exhibition on 1867 – that brought the need for developments in engineering education to the fore (Buchanan 1989). A key figure in the development of engineering science as a bridge between theory and practice is William John Macquorn Rankine, though 'the initial response to the Rankine system was cautious' (Buchanan 1989, 170). It was during periods of development and expansion for the HE system that engineering education was able to gain a steadier foothold in the academy. Based on a compromise between the need for theoretical competence and the British engineering tradition of apprenticeship, engineering education was fully established in British universities by 1914 (Buchanan 1989).

Severn (2009) argues that during the twentieth century, there were important contextual changes in the HE sector that influenced the landscape of engineering education; the publication of the Robbins Report in 1963, which emphasised the expansion of HE and recommended that Colleges of Advance Technology should become universities; and Britain's accession to the European Economic Community (EEC) in 1973, which led to the introduction of the MEng (Masters of Engineering) course to UK engineering education and greater standardisation of course content in order to allow greater transferability across Europe (see also New Civil Engineer 2009). Currently, there are plans in universities in the UK to develop an interdisciplinary engineering curriculum, for example, with business or environmental sciences, and innovative teaching and assessment methods, which form a continuation of earlier progress made in engineering education and reflect developments in HE more widely (Borrego and Cutler 2010; Lueddeke 2010).

More recent developments – innovations in content and delivery

The most frequently referred-to concepts with regard to innovation in engineering curriculum are the introduction of interdisciplinary (or multidisciplinary) aspects to engineering courses (see, for example, Cotgrave 2005; Harrison, Macpherson, and Williams 2007; Ivins 1997; Markes 2006; Skates 2003; Spinks, Silburn, and Birchall 2007), although these terms are not interchangeable and denote differing philosophical foundations to the inclusion of non-technical content on engineering programmes. Here, we can delineate differing conceptual approaches, broadly summarised as (1) interdisciplinary: programmes that allow students to study content offered across different departments (2) multidisciplinary (may also be termed pluridisciplinary or transdisciplinary): broadly where students/teaching staff incorporate non-engineering learning into the curriculum, or (3) a-disciplinary: the incorporation of content/pedagogical style that transcends traditional disciplinary boundaries, hence applicable in some way for most HE students. In the UK, this is often defined as 'transferable skills'. In research that uses interdisciplinarity as a focus for empirical study, it is helpful to be mindful of these differing concepts.

There is a general agreement that interdisciplinary, multidisciplinary or holistic approaches in engineering courses are a positive step (see Barnard et al. 2012a). Cotgrave (2005) argues that a 'holistic' approach to developing design solutions, the ability to appreciate the broad range of professions within the sector and develop a wider appreciation of the context in which engineers work, is crucial (see also Richter and Paretti 2009). A more holistic education is argued to make students better engineers in practice. However, the requirements for gaining chartered status are set by the professional accreditation bodies, which makes including interdisciplinary modules to an already packed programme of study problematic (Powell et al. 2004, see also Winberg 2008).

The driving force for skills development in the engineering sector is linked to productivity levels, an identified skills shortage and a focus upon the skills the industry needs (Barnard et al. 2012a). Markes' (2006) review of employability skills in the UK engineering sector reveals the need for adaptability, flexibility, good communication skills and teamwork, all of which relate to the disciplinary flexibility and transferable skills of engineering students. The requirements of industry are increasingly dominant in the UK as student employability and the utility of a university degree are at the forefront of students' minds in making choices about where and what to study, especially since the introduction of tuition fees in 1998. The development of interdisciplinary engineering education based upon a broad definition of curriculum is also a product of closer relationships between universities and employers.

Other research that focuses on the benefits of interdisciplinary developments is described by Harrison, Macpherson, and Williams (2007) who argue that interdisciplinary collaboration is critical for UK engineers. Harrison, Macpherson, and Williams (2007) found that some companies experienced 'skills gaps', where time and money was spent getting graduates up to speed with the requirements of the job. They argue that engineering is traditionally 'mono-disciplinary' – encouraging specialist technical knowledge and a strong identification with own discipline – at the expense of broader knowledge/skills and appreciation of other disciplines. As graduates will often go on to work in 'multi-functional' teams (in larger companies) or themselves adopt a wider spectrum of roles (in smaller companies), a mono-disciplinary approach does not adequately prepare engineers for this 'reality'. Spinks, Silburn, and Birchall (2007) note an emphasis on the multi-faceted nature of contemporary engineering work and on the need to understand the whole range of input that results in the success of a project. Thus, the widening of the experience and skills of engineers can be conceived as a response to wider changes in society and engineering organizations.

Methodology

In order to explore the nature and experience of interdisciplinary education, we adopted a mixed method approach, combining curriculum analysis and interviews with students. In the UK, Civil Engineering is the third highest engineering subject area by student enrolments (following Mechanical and Electrical and Electronic Engineering), with 4796 students accepted onto Civil Engineering degree programmes in 2010 (UCAS 2011). Within the broad Civil Engineering subject area, there are approximately 300 programmes delivered in the UK. In order to focus our analysis on the extent of interdisciplinary content in civil engineering curriculum, we concentrate upon programmes at the MEng level that are delivered at 40 HE institutions in the UK. In order to provide a full picture, we collected data on at least one MEng programme at each institution that provides MEng programmes in Civil Engineering.

The curriculum analysis was an important part of the research as this allowed a deeper understanding of what is taught, prior to interrogating students' experiences and responses to such an education via one-to-one interviews. This follows the work of Bernstein (1971) who looked at the codes of framing of knowledge and how students/staff are socialised into a subject and later Bird (2001) who argues for a sociology of academic curriculum that questions what is taught and why. Bird (2001) suggests that most attention on curriculum focuses on the 'how' rather than 'what' question and therefore, little is known about what is taught and how disciplines are defined and maintained. Bernstein's notion of classification is useful for thinking about what happens when you attempt to weaken the boundaries between disciplines in order to create interdisciplinarity, raising questions about power relations and the interests served in changes to academic boundaries. Ultimately, educational fields can be viewed as arenas of practice and sites of contestation, conflict and struggle with regard to meaning and power (Bernstein 1999). As Bernstein's analysis of education and knowledge brings to the fore the principles of social control and expressions of power, we may look closer at the development of interdisciplinary education, in this case, in engineering, and perceive that changes in HE reflect trends evident more widely in society.

In this research, we focus on identifying interdisciplinary content in the civil engineering curriculum, which was broadly defined as 'non-technical'. The delivery of innovative programmes is not always easily separated from innovative pedagogy, and the difficulties associated with how to define interdisciplinary content are raised during the research. Through curriculum analysis, we can uncover the details of what is taught and begin to understand the complex interplay between differing 'modes' of learning students digest over the course of their study. Moore and Young (2001) discuss the dominance of two competing ideologies with regard to curriculum; 'neo-conservative traditionalism' and 'technical instrumentalists', these kind of metanarratives amongst others may be played out in the interaction between the profession and the academy, at faculty level, between students and teachers, but also can be found in the curriculum itself – what is taught and why. These debates are also explored in the interviews with students.

Interviews were conducted with students at four different institutions in order to explore how the curriculum content is experienced and perceived. The interviewees were accessed in liaison with the staff in the academic department in which their programme was based. In total, 24 interviews with students took place at 4 HE institutions – with 12 female and 12 male students. Semi-structured interviews allowed an exploration of various aspects of students' decision-making processes and experiences on their programme of study.

Curriculum analysis

Accessing data

Less than half of institutions looked at had detailed curriculum information freely available on their websites at that time (April–June 2010); in order to access this information to perform the curriculum analysis, it was necessary to contact 24 institutions directly (39 institutions in total were looked at). This was carried out with varied success. Some institutions would not provide the curriculum information necessary to identify interdisciplinary content (see Table 1).

Once the curriculum details were available, the process for analysing content began by looking closely at the module titles and descriptions – does the module have a focus on non-technical education? Does the module offer a more contextual analysis of civil engineering? Does the module contain non-engineering content? For modules that we could answer yes, a note was made of the credit for this module and analysis was performed for overall scores and the interdisciplinary content within each year and for the whole programme.

In the context of this study, interdisciplinary content was found under a variety of guises. Examples of modules that we considered added interdisciplinary content to programmes include: Economics and Structure of Industry; Philosophy; Rights and Wrongs: The Engineering Profession and Society; The Aesthetics of Design; Languages; Business and Management Studies; Teamwork and Leadership; Organisational Theory and Behaviour; Finance; Law and Contracts; Sustainable Development and the Environment; also, modules that have transferable skills as their focus – developing communication skills, etc.

Results

The curriculum analysis shows that there are relatively low levels of interdisciplinary content in civil engineering curriculum in the UK. This is consistent across all years for all institutions as the mean data shows around 13–15 percent. A more detailed look at the results shows that some institutions have a greater amount of interdisciplinary content: for example, Birmingham; Brunel; Coventry; Dundee; University College London and Warwick. In particular, we can see that the Civil Engineering programme offered at an institution such as Warwick had significantly higher levels of interdisciplinary content due to the fact that the first-year programme is a general engineering programme that allows students a wider curriculum before a greater emphasis on civil engineering in later years. Institutions that offered less interdisciplinary content were: Bath; Durham; Edinburgh Napier; and Salford. The curriculum analysis differentiates between levels of interdisciplinarity by first year of programme, or second year and later, which allows for a more nuanced examination of the ways in which this kind of content is incorporated into more mainstream curriculum. For example, the MEng programme at Glasgow University has above average interdisciplinary content in the first year (21%) but offers none at all for the rest of the programme, whilst Coventry University has below average content in the first year, yet incorporates much more interdisciplinary content in the later years of the programme (35%). The analysis conducted presents an interesting starting point for a discussion about how this kind of content is

Table 1. Percentage of interdisciplinary content by institution and year of programme.

Institution	MEng programme	% Interdisciplinary content		
		Year 1	Year 2+	Total
Aberdeen	Civil and Environmental Engineering	0	15	12
Bath	Civil Engineering	5	9	8
Bath	Civil and Architectural Engineering	5	9	8
Birmingham	Civil Engineering	17	25	23
Bradford	Civil and Structural Engineering	17	14	15
Brighton	Civil Engineering	17	19	19
Bristol	Civil Engineering	8	15	14
Brunel	Civil Engineering with Sustainability	33	19	23
Cardiff	Civil Engineering	8	10	10
City	Civil Engineering	8	20	16
Coventry	Civil Engineering	8	35	28
Dundee	Civil Engineering	33	17	19
Durham	Civil Engineering	17	7	9
Edinburgh	Civil Engineering	12	15	14
Edinburgh	Civil and Environmental Engineering	12	15	14
Edinburgh	Civil Engineering with Construction Management	12	17	16
Napier	Civil Engineering	0	11	9
Napier	Civil and Transportation Engineering	0	11	9
Exeter	Civil Engineering	12	19	17
Glasgow	Civil Engineering	21	0	4
Greenwich	Civil Engineering	–	–	–
Heriot-Watt	Civil Engineering	12	11	11
Imperial	Civil Engineering	25	10	14
Leeds	Civil and Structural Engineering	12	12	12
Leeds	Civil and Environmental Engineering	12	15	13
Liverpool	Civil Engineering	6	19	16
Liverpool	Civil and Structural Engineering	6	19	16
Loughborough	Civil Engineering	10	21	19
Manchester	Civil Engineering	25	8	16
Newcastle	Civil Engineering	0	25	19
Northumbria	Building Services Engineering	0	14	10
Nottingham	Civil Engineering	25	15	18
Oxford	Civil Engineering	–	–	–
Plymouth	Civil Engineering	–	–	–
Portsmouth	Civil Engineering	8	19	17
Queens	Civil Engineering	–	–	–
Salford	Civil Engineering	17	7	9
Sheffield	Civil Engineering	17	17	17
Sheffield	Civil and Structural Engineering	17	17	17
Southampton	Civil Engineering	0	17	13
Southampton	Environmental Engineering	0	15	11
Strathclyde	Civil Engineering	–	–	–
Surrey	Civil Engineering	4	17	14
Swansea	Civil Engineering	17	8	10
Ulster	Civil Engineering	12	21	19
UCL	Civil Engineering	25	23	23
Warwick	Civil Engineering	62	27	36
UK mean data	–	13	15	15

included in the curriculum and how there are many different approaches in teaching what appears to be on the surface the same degree programme.

Student interviews

We conducted interviews with students that explored their decision to study civil engineering, experiences on the programme and views on what is taught. As a talking point in the interviews, we produced condensed versions of their own degree curriculum and one for another institution for them to read through and discuss. This enabled the student to make comparisons between curriculum content, which turned out to be a fruitful way of gaining an insight into their opinions about what is suitable to be taught on a civil engineering programme.

Participants were asked to reflect upon the factors that impacted on their decision to study the civil engineering discipline and embark upon their programme of study. For the majority of respondents, peers and family are influential with regard to decisions about where and what to study – for these civil engineering students in particular, family were cited as being generally supportive, though sometimes uninformed about what civil engineering is. Our findings reflect findings of other research that outlines the importance of familial and peer influence on HE choice (see Breakwell, Fife-shaw, and Devereux 1988; Reay et al. 2001; Brooks 2003; David et al. 2003; Barnard et al. 2012b). Many of the respondents spoke about key family members who emphasise the idea that maths/sciences are 'proper' subjects, thus directly and indirectly influencing these students' decision to study an engineering subject. This reflects a general perception about suitable areas of study that does not drill down to the level of curriculum content: the programme title/subject area is enough. It is the idea of what a subject is, rather than an explicit knowledge of programme content, that is influential. It is presumed that a 'proper' sounding subject like civil engineering will entail a 'proper' education. One student describes how she came to be doing civil engineering:

> I think it was at A Levels and it was by absolute chance because I wanted to go into drama but I was really good at maths and physics and my teacher rang me up and said, "Are you sure you want to do this? Are you sure you don't want to go into something a bit more substantial?" So in my GCSE years I got told that engineering is probably the best thing for me to do. I wanted to do architecture initially and when I got researching engineering it took my fancy. A lot of research on the internet and then I decided that's definitely what I wanted to do and that's how I came about it. (DF2)

Non-content based reasons given for taking a particular study programme were equally prevalent across all respondents: they include reputation of institution, location of institution (i.e. to live nearer home to keep living costs low), perception of campus, support, influence of friends and family. Previous research on student choice of HE programme has found motivations for choice to be highly based upon socio-economic background, those from working-class or ethnic minorities taking particular aspects into account in their decision-making (for a more detailed discussion see Reay et al. 2001; Dawes and Brown 2005; Voigt 2007; Davies et al. 2012). In this study, factors influencing the specialism chosen in civil engineering include: being an 'outdoors person'; having an interest in structures (but a 'proper' subject i.e. maths/science based, unlike the more 'arty' architecture); choice of A-Level subjects and perception of good career prospects.

Various reasons emerged as influencing students' choice of programme. For some students, the choices are limited to what is available once the grades have been published: 'I went through clearing so didn't have much choice of where to go' (DM1). Most participants responded that course content was not influential in their decision to take a particular study programme. Many students knew they wanted to study civil engineering, but made the decision between potential programmes of study on other factors (such as university ranking, location, the opportunity to do a year in industry, etc.). One response that is common amongst the respondents was a student who said that he did not look into course content, as he knew he wanted to do civil engineering (DM2). Another respondent commented that: 'I wasn't really sure what the university course would contain and we didn't get much information on it' (AF3). A few respondents had previous knowledge of course content as they had an older sibling or friend doing the course, but on the whole, it seems the students lack knowledge of what they will study until they are studying it.

In terms of students' experiences of the curriculum, they acknowledged the MEng Civil Engineering as a 'broad' education that highlights the importance of knowledge of other *engineering* disciplines, the need to include transferable skills and group project work to reflect professional working practices. A step beyond the perception of civil engineering as a relatively 'open' discipline is the inclusion of interdisciplinary content: what did students think about this? In general, both male and female students reported being initially surprised by the presence of non-technical content (e.g. management); however, most respondents appreciated the non-technical content later in their degree, particularly those that undertook an industrial placement. One respondent commented on a business and management module: 'they've definitely given me quite an insight into actually how the business and the other side of construction works, which was something that on my year out was picked up as a weakness of mine' (AM3). Another respondent questions the inclusion of interdisciplinary content on his programme:

> For me, I can't understand why that's there as part of the civil's module. And then even a Modern Foreign Language – okay, sometimes you get stuff with a language extra. Then Rights and Wrongs of the Engineering Profession Society – yeah, that seems relevant as a first year module. But then Introduction to Ancient Philosophy – to me, I don't think it's specific to a civil engineering course. (DM1)

However, some respondents noted a change in perceptions towards interdisciplinary content over time, with students nearing the end of the MEng reporting a greater understanding of the necessity of this kind of education to prepare for the world of work. As one respondent states:

> I didn't really realize there would be so much construction management, project management, finance management. And to me, well at the beginning I didn't think that was civil engineering, and obviously I am in my last year now and I realize you do need to understand it. But at the beginning I was a bit like 'whoa! This isn't civil engineering'. (AF2)

An interesting finding was that some found the non-technical modules more difficult as they were out of their 'comfort zone'. As well as a discussion of the programme on which respondents were studying, they were asked to look over a summary of an alternative curriculum from another institution. Some respondents questioned the narrower curriculum and prefer the broader curriculum:

> I think our programme tends to make you more sellable to other people as well, you could go into a different industry and you would have transferable skills. Whereas with the one from the other university tends to be more technical. (AF3)

Conversely, some questioned the technical ability of those students on the more interdisciplinary programme, suggesting that the inclusion of interdisciplinary content is at the expense of important technical education. This view is mirrored in Alpay's (2012) discussion of the development of general engineering programmes in the UK, which highlights that 'some institutions may view direct specialisation as a competitive edge or niche over other equivalent (e.g. research-intensive) institutions offering general engineering' (Alpay 2012, 10). Further, in our study, many students stated that they preferred the more technical programme. Overall, we found a mixed picture with regard to student perceptions of interdisciplinary content.

Discussion: contestations of knowledge and informational transparency

The context of the institutions that provide engineering HE and the influence of industry on such programmes may constrain change in the curriculum when tied closely with 'traditional' cultures and norms, even in universities where interdisciplinarity is a specified goal (Pharo et al. 2012). Bagilhole and Goode (1998) found that in male-dominated disciplines, such as engineering, a 'narrow' definition of the term 'curriculum' was predominantly in use. This features strongly defined appropriate discipline content and an unproblematic body of knowledge (McKenna and Yalvac 2007). A recent study by Alpay (2012) on student attraction to flexibility and breadth in engineering curriculum found that a general engineering programme that offers the opportunity to specialise later in the degree programme to be a good option for students who were considering doing a degree. In the same study, it was found that students indicated the importance of non-technical content; 'four common items appeared amongst the top six rankings: leadership; teamwork; business skills; self-awareness and personal development' (Alpay 2012, 9). Thus, the tradition of engineering that focuses upon 'technical' skills is in conflict, not only with people who do not identify with a technical discipline, but also with prospective students themselves and the modern take on the multi-dimensional engineering professional.

The difficulties found in accessing curriculum information and the students' lack of knowledge of curriculum prior to study demonstrates that there is a need for greater transparency that goes beyond superficial information, which would allow future students to learn more about the curriculum and find a programme of study that matches their interests. KIS present greater possibilities for this to happen; however, proposals for KIS do not include detailed information on programme content, instead concentrating on easily comparable and visual information: for example, figures on contact time and employability.

It is important to acknowledge the *potential* for greater information available on curriculum content to be counterproductive to initiatives that develop interdisciplinary education – as students who are set on studying, civil engineering, for example, do not necessarily want interdisciplinary content. The idea of greater openness and availability of information follows general trends in HE in the UK around the publication of performance indicators that are aimed at providing prospective students information from which they are able to make choices about where and what to study, but these tend to be focused on delivery of education and outcomes rather than the content of degree programmes: a focus on the 'how' and 'outcomes' of learning, rather than the 'what' question. Respondents in this research demonstrated a significant lack of detailed knowledge about the content of the programme of study prior to enrolment, but also ambivalence towards non-technical content: this leads to questions about how far universities may innovate curricula when student (and family) *expectations* are firmly rooted at the heart of the traditional discipline. As Strathern (2000) notes, there may be unintended consequences to greater transparency and the use of performance indicators in individual and organizational decision-making.

Conclusions

This article outlined our findings on the prevalence of interdisciplinary curriculum in civil engineering in the UK and the views and experiences of students with regard to this kind of education. We found that universities currently operate a varied approach to transparency regarding curriculum with less than half of institutions making detailed curriculum information freely available on their websites. The introduction of KIS provides an opportunity for more easily accessible information on curricula, but mainly focuses on mode of delivery, services to students and outcomes. Taking into account Strathern (2000) and others' reservations about increasing transparency in HE, we suggest that if students do not have the opportunity for learning more about what they will be expected to study (not just the 'how' but the 'what' question), we can assume that curriculum is something that informs experience, but not decisions about which programme of study to embark upon. Moves towards interdisciplinary education, not only in civil engineering, but across the engineering faculty and beyond, may or may not be welcomed by students wanting a purely technical education, and may come as a surprise to those not previously informed of curriculum content. The boundaries of what is considered to be interdisciplinary will differ according to subject area and as such offers an interesting window into sites of struggle for meaning and power in academic pedagogy (Bernstein 1970). The research presented here offers an interesting starting point for a discussion about how this kind of content is developed, communicated to and experienced by students.

Acknowledgements

The research leading to these results has received funding from the European Commission's Seventh Framework Programme FP7/2007–2013 under grant agreement no 230376 – research project HELENA (Higher Education leading to Engineering and Scientific Careers). The authors gratefully acknowledge the support of the EC. The authors would like to thank the interview participants for their input and the time of departmental staff at the four institutions who helped to promote the project to their students. The authors would also like to thank anonymous reviewers for their comments on a draft of the article.

References

Alpay, E. 2012. "Student Attraction to Engineering through Flexibility and Breadth in the Curriculum." *European Journal of Engineering Education* 2012: 1–19. doi:10.1080/03043797.2012.742870.

Bagilhole, B., and J. Goode. 1998. "The 'Gender Dimension' of Both the 'Narrow' and 'Broad' Curriculum in UK Higher Education: Do Women Lose Out in Both?" *Gender and Education* 10 (4): 445–458. doi:10.1080/09540259820862.

Barnard, S., B. Bagilhole, A. Dainty, and T. Hassan. 2012a. "Women, Engineering and Higher Education in the UK: Trends in Participation and Curriculum Development." In *Gender and Interdisciplinary Education for Engineers. Does Interdisciplinary Education Improve the Gender Balance and Attract more Young People in Engineering and Technology Higher Education*? Proceedings of the GIEE HELENA Conference, Paris, June 23–24, edited by A. Béraud, A.-S. Godfroy, and J. Michel, 65–78. Rotterdam: Sense.

Barnard, S., T. Hassan, B. Bagilhole, and A. Dainty. 2012b. "'They're Not Girly Girls': An Exploration of Quantitative and Qualitative Data on Engineering and Gender in Higher Education." *European Journal of Engineering Education* 37 (2): 193–204. doi:10.1080/03043797.2012.661702.

BBC. 2011. "Students to Get Best-buy Facts and Consumer Rights." *BBC*. Accessed June 24, 2012. http://www.bbc.co.uk/news/education-13874483.

Bernstein, B. 1971. "On the Classification and Framing of Educational Knowledge." In *Knowledge and Control: New Directions for the Sociology of Education*, edited by M. F. D. Young, 245–270. London: Collier Macmillan.

Bernstein, B. 1999. "Vertical and Horizontal Discourse: An Essay." *British Journal of Sociology of Education* 20 (2): 157–173. doi:10.1080/01425699995380.

Bird, E. 2001. "Disciplining the Interdisciplinary: Radicalism and the Academic Curriculum." *British Journal of Sociology of Education* 22 (4): 463–478. doi:10.1080/01425690120094430.

Borrego, M., and S. Cutler. 2010. "Constructive Alignment of Interdisciplinary Graduate Curriculum in Engineering and Science: An Analysis of Successful IGERT Proposals." *Journal of Engineering Education* 99 (4): 355–369. doi:10.1002/j.2168-9830.2010.tb01068.x.

Breakwell, G. M., C. Fife-Schaw, and J. Devereux. 1988. "Parental Influence and Teenagers' Motivation to Train for Technological Jobs." *Journal of Occupational Psychology* 61 (1): 79–88. doi:10.1111/j.2044-8325.1988.tb00273.x.

Brooks, R. 2003. "Young People's Higher Education Choices: The Role of Family and Friends." *British Journal of Sociology of Education* 24 (3): 283–297. doi:10.1080/01425690301896.

Buchanan, R. A. 1989. *The Engineers: A History of the Engineering Profession in Britain, 1750–1914*. London: Jessica Kingsley.

Cotgrave, A. 2005. "Tuning the Undergraduate Construction Curriculum: Embedding Health, Safety and Environmental Issues in Order to Improve Employability." *Transactions* 2 (1): 28–43. doi:10.11120/tran.2005.02010028.

David, M. E., S. J. Ball, J. Davies, and D. Reay. 2003. "Gender Issues in Parental Involvement in Student Choices of Higher Education." *Gender and Education* 15 (1): 21–36. doi:10.1080/0954025032000042121.

Davies, P. 2012. "Can Governments Improve Higher Education Through 'Informing Choice'?" *British Journal of Educational Studies* 60 (3): 261–276. doi:10.1080/00071005.2012.715626.

Davies, P., J. Mangan, A. Hughes, and K. Slack. 2012. "Labour Market Motivation and Undergraduates' Choice of Degree Subject." *British Educational Research Journal* 39 (2): 361–382. doi:10.1080/01411926.2011.646239.

Dawes, P. L., and J. Brown 2005. "The Composition of Consideration and Choice Sets in Undergraduate University Choice: An Exploratory Study." *Journal of Marketing for Higher Education* 14 (2): 37–59. doi:10.1300/J050v14n02_03.

Gregory, M. S. 1971. *History and Development of Engineering*. London: Longman.

Harrison, G. P., D. E. Macpherson, and D. A. Williams. 2007. "Promoting Interdisciplinarity in Engineering Teaching." *European Journal of Engineering Education* 32 (3): 285–293. doi:10.1080/03043790701276775.

HEFCE. 2012a. "Key Information Sets." Accessed December 28, 2012. http://www.hefce.ac.uk/whatwedo/lt/publicinfo/kis/.

HEFCE. 2012b. "PIs: An Introduction." Accessed December 28, 2012. http://www.hesa.ac.uk/index.php?option=com_content&task=view&id=2073&Itemid=141.

Ivins, J. R. 1997. "Interdisciplinary Project Work: Practice Makes Perfect?" *IEEE Transactions on Education* 40 (3): 179–183. doi:10.1109/13.618027.

Lueddeke, G. 2010. "Curriculum Matters: Building Capacity for Strategic Change in UK Higher Education." *International Journal of Strategic Change Management* 2 (1): 18–31. doi:10.1504/IJSCM.2010.032520.

Markes, I. 2006. "A Review of Literature on Employability Skill Needs in Engineering." *European Journal of Engineering Education* 31 (6): 637–650. doi:10.1080/03043790600911704.

McKenna, A. F., and B. Yalvac. 2007. "Characterizing Engineering Faculty's Teaching Approaches." *Teaching in Higher Education* 12 (3): 405–418. doi:10.1080/13562510701278765.

Moore, R., and M. Young. 2001. "Knowledge and the Curriculum in the Sociology of Education: Towards a Reconceptualisation." *British Journal of Sociology of Education* 22 (4): 445–461. doi:10.1080/01425690120094421.

New Civil Engineer. 2009. "Engineering Education has Come a Long Way Over a Long Time." *New Civil Engineer.* Accessed May 21, 2012. http://www.nce.co.uk/news/ice/engineering-education-has-come-a-long-way-over-a-long-time/5202408.article.

Pharo, E. J., A. Davison, K. Warr, M. Nursey-Bray, K. Beswick, E. Wapstra, and C. Jones. 2012. "Can Teacher Collaboration Overcome Barriers to Interdisciplinary Learning in a Disciplinary University? A Case Study Using Climate Change." *Teaching in Higher Education* 17 (5): 497–507. doi:10.1080/13562517.2012.658560.

Powell, A., B. Bagilhole, A. Dainty, and R. Neale. 2004. "Does the Engineering Culture in UK Higher Education Advance Women's Careers." *Equal Opportunities International* 23 (7/8): 21–38. doi:10.1108/02610150410787882.

Pugh, G., G. Coates, and N. Adnett. 2005. "Performance Indicators and Widening Participation in UK Higher Education." *Higher Education Quarterly* 59 (1): 19–39. doi:10.1111/j.1468-2273.2005.00279.x.

Reay, D., J. Davies, M. David, and S. J. Ball. 2001. "Choices of Degree or Degrees of Choice? Class, 'Race' and the Higher Education Choice Process." *Sociology* 35: 855. doi:10.1177/0038038501035004004.

Richter, D. M., and M. C. Paretti. 2009. "Identifying Barriers to and Outcomes of Interdisciplinarity in the Engineering Classroom." *European Journal of Engineering Education* 34 (1): 29–45. doi:10.1080/03043790802710185.

Severn, R. T. 2009. *The Development of the Faculty of Engineering at the University of Bristol 1909–2009: A History to Mark Its Centenary.* Bristol: University of Bristol. http://www.ima.org.uk/news/rt_severn.html.

Skates, G. W. 2003. "Interdisciplinary Project Working in Engineering Education." *European Journal of Engineering Education* 28 (2): 187–201. doi:10.1080/0304379031000079022.

Spinks, N., N. L. J. Silburn, and D. W. Birchall. 2007. "Making it All Work: The Engineering Graduate of the Future, a UK Perspective." *European Journal of Engineering Education* 32 (3): 325–335. doi:10.1080/03043790701278573.

Strathern, M. 2000. "The Tyranny of Transparency." *British Educational Research Journal* 26 (3): 309–321. doi:10.1080/713651562.

Tsoukas, H. 1997. "The Tyranny of Light: The Temptations and Paradoxes of the Information Society." *Futures* 29 (9): 827–843. doi:10.1016/S0016-3287(97)00035-9.

UCAS. 2011. *Online Statistics on Student Applications and Acceptances by Subject.* www.ucas.ac.uk.

Voigt, K. 2007. "Individual Choice and Unequal Participation in Higher Education." *Theory and Research in Education* 5 (1): 87–112. doi:10.1177/1477878507073617.

Winberg, C. 2008. "Teaching Engineering/Engineering Teaching: Interdisciplinary Collaboration and the Construction of Academic Identities." *Teaching in Higher Education* 13 (3): 353–367. doi:10.1080/13562510802045394.

Chinese students making sense of problem-based learning and Western teaching – pitfalls and coping strategies

Malene Gram, Kirsten Jæger, Junyang Liu, Li Qing and Xiangying Wu

Department of Culture and Global Studies, Aalborg University, Aalborg, Denmark; Department of Culture and Communication, University of International Relations, Beijing, China; English Department, University of International Relations, Beijing, China; Department of International Economics and Trade, University of International Relations, Beijing, China

Culturally different imaginations of student and teacher roles, incongruent perceptions of academic standards, and diverging conceptualizations of learning may cause 'difficult times' for institutions and individual learners involved in international education. Universities practicing alternative approaches to teaching and learning, for example problem-based learning (PBL), may face even larger challenges because of the unfamiliarity of international students with such approaches. This study explores the difficult times experienced by Chinese students in a PBL setting at a Danish University. The main result of the study is an increased understanding of these students' remarkable 'survival' skills, coping strategies, and learning outcomes gained from the challenging immersion in a Danish PBL environment.

Introduction

'Making sense of teaching in difficult times' can be understood from several perspectives, including the perspective of the individual student. This article takes the perspective of Chinese students who go abroad to study in a radically different educational system and investigates how these students experience and cope with the difficulties they encounter.

The research literature draws a bleak picture of Chinese students studying in the Western world and focuses on differing learning styles, a passive attitude in lectures (Chen, Bennett, and Maton 2008), and a lack of contact with domestic students (Brunette et al. 2011). Chinese students do not integrate with domestic students but often mingle with other Chinese students and, consequently, fail to improve their language skills (Bartlett and Fischer 2011) and to build friendships with students who are not from their own national group. Such friendships are found to improve the level of satisfaction (Hendrickson, Rosen, and Aune 2011) and improve acculturation, and psychosocial adjustment (Zhang and Goodson 2011). In their study of Chinese engineering students, Du and Hansen (2005) found that Chinese students in Denmark need to deal with a number of practical issues, e.g. cooking, transport, and appointments with group members and supervisors. Furthermore, they are surprised by the directness of student/teacher interaction, and they are overwhelmed by experiencing Danish students interrupting teachers and supervisors and not necessarily following the supervisors' advice (Du and Hansen 2005).

In addition to investigating Chinese students' study experience in a Western university, this article addresses Chinese students' experience of problem-based learning (PBL) and group work, where students are expected to be active and reflective, and to challenge both teachers and textbooks. If the sinister picture sketched in current research literature holds true, it could be anticipated that it would be very difficult for Chinese students to transfer into a PBL system, where all their known points of orientation are out of play.

The topic of Chinese students abroad has mainly been studied through quantitative approaches (e.g. Wang and Moore 2007; Zhang and Goodson 2011; exceptions are Du and Hansen 2005; Brunette et al. 2011), and mainly in Anglo-American-Australian settings (Brunette et al. 2011; Selvarajah 2006; exceptions are Du and Hansen 2005). In order to gain access to the students' own view of the PBL experience, this study takes a qualitative approach. The article builds on the international research literature on the 'Chinese learner' and on a data sample consisting of in-depth interviews and essays authored by Chinese students studying at a Danish University.

The authors are aware of the considerable risk of simplifying intercultural complexities when engaging the experience of a specific national group. Thus, promoting an intercultural dialog around the topic of internationalization of education and the ensuing encounters of educational philosophies, practices, and cultures would be a desirable outcome of this study.

Background

The influence of Confucian heritage on education in China has attracted the interest of both Western and Chinese educational scholars (McMahon 2011; Chan and Rao 2010; Wu 2011). According to Wu, principles of teaching and learning are central to Confucian philosophy. The influence of Confucianism on education dates back to 200 BCE (Deng 2011), when Confucianism inspired the building of a national system for the education of civil servants. The training was based on the learning of classic Chinese philosophy and literature (Deng 2011). Confucian educational ideas were actively fought as an obstacle to modernity by the 4 May 1919 movement, introducing modern Western concepts such as 'democracy' and 'nation' in Chinese educational discourse, and generally striving for a democratization of Chinese education (Deng 2011, 562). The influence of Maoism on the educational system comprised of two phases: first, the educational system was thoroughly revised according to Soviet Marxist principles (Wu 2011, 583), second, a move toward a highly standardized and thoroughly regulated educational system. The relinquishment of Soviet and all other forms of foreign influence during the Cultural Revolution also involved a break with all remains of Chinese cultural traditions such as Confucianism. Deng Xiaoping led China through a period of pragmatism and increasing openness toward Western ideas. Thus, according to Wu, Confucian philosophy became influenced by Western and globalized mindsets. In the Confucian tradition, the ultimate purpose of education is the self-perfection of the individual, and the development toward this goal is understood as the Way (the *dao*) to an ever deepening understanding of oneself and one's role in the world. According to the Confucian tradition, the study of classic texts helps the individual to find and follow the Way but in ways differing considerably from Western modes of engaging philosophical texts. What is important in the reading of Confucian philosophy is the interpretation or the form of resonance that this reading produces in the individual, not the learning of the words and the texts themselves. When texts are memorized, it is in order to produce such a personal translation or 'effect', not in order to learn the words of the texts by heart. The purpose of memorizing is to be able to forget the words but hold on to the interpretation or 'effect' of the words on one's personality (Wu 2011).

Western scholars' descriptions of the Confucian tradition and its influence on Chinese higher education (HE) learners indicate the difficulty of appreciating culturally different epistemological traditions and educational practices (e.g. Biggs 1998). Thus, several scholars recognize that the learning behavior of Chinese learners deviates from the practices and values of Western HE students. Parts of the literature holding this position depict Chinese learners as generally authoritarian and passive learners disinclined to let their own voices be heard in classroom contexts. Passive and authoritarian behavior is ascribed to the influence of a collectivist culture emphasizing social harmony rather than the unfolding of individual personalities. Chinese learners have also been depicted as 'rote learners' rarely achieving knowledge levels beyond that of surface learning.

According to Wang and Moore (2007) perceiving Chinese students as a homogeneous group has generated a number of simplifying stereotypes regarding Chinese students' learning styles. They find that some writers propose that Asian and Western learners hold differing pedagogical preferences:

> Western learners accept involvement and learning through their own discovery and exploration. Chinese learners expect the teacher to lead and provide learning points, and they prefer a passive approach to learning. (Wang and Moore 2007, 32)

However, being passive in class does not equal lack of learning, and rote learning does not equal surface learning (Wang and Moore 2007; Chalmers and Volet 1997). The observed differences between Western and Chinese/Confucian Heritage student behavior have been subject to misinterpretations but seem to have a foundation in culture-specific cognitive models of concepts of learning and education (Li 2003; McMahon 2011).

A rising number of Chinese students now study abroad, and differences in pedagogical and cultural backgrounds cause difficulties (Kirby 2008; Selvarajah 2006). Thus, Asian students are found to have a difficult time:

> These students are found to experience disproportionately high levels of academic dissatisfaction, stress, and general adaptation problems during their stay in foreign countries. (Selvarajah 2006, 144)

Chinese learning behavior is often judged by Western standards and found wanting in terms of active participation and critical thinking abilities (McMahon 2011). As the notions of active participation and critical thinking are central to PBL, Chinese students may find PBL environments particularly challenging. PBL is generally understood as learning of academic content with a point of departure in a problem. Learning is student-directed (organized, managed, and controlled by the students themselves), interdisciplinary, and often group-organized. Teachers function as facilitators and supervisors, not as lecturers or 'information-providers'. Learning is typically organized in projects, involving a goal, a timeframe, and a set of operations and methods (Kolmos 1996).

In the early 1970s, two PBL universities were established in Denmark. One of these universities hosts the study programs of the students participating in this study. The inauguration of these universities reflected, first of all, the need to make university education more accessible and, second, the interest in educational forms that would foster competences suitable for the emergent knowledge economy (Illeris 1981). The overarching principle for organizing, teaching, and learning at the new universities was PBL. Forerunners of PBL initiatives had been limited to specific departments or programs. Introducing PBL as a *national* political initiative required the new universities to organize all programs according to PBL principles, regardless of the disciplinary traditions.

In the establishment of a theoretical foundation for PBL-organized education, Critical Theory and thus Western Enlightenment thinking played a predominant role (Illeris 1981; Kolmos 1996). For example, Illeris' concept of 'counter-qualification' refers to concurrent processes of competence-building and social criticism, emerging as consequences of 'enlightening' and consciousness-raising learning processes driven by the exploration of socially pertinent problems. More pragmatic tenets were advocated during the 1980s and 1990s (de Graaff and Kolmos 2007).

PBL proved to be an efficient mode of organizing HE. The PBL candidates developed strong collaboration and organization skills, and compared to traditional university candidates, they came across as creative and independent problem-solvers. To a higher extent than traditional educational forms, PBL allows the students to engage topics which have a personal appeal to them, and within broad interdisciplinary programs, students' sense of personal relevance may take precedence over traditional disciplinary goals (such as specific syllabi). The degrees of freedom vary from program to program and from semester to semester but are generally higher than in traditional university education.

Methodological considerations

To capture Chinese students' own experiences of being students abroad in a Western PBL university, a qualitative and interpretive approach to data collection and analysis was chosen (Kvale 1996).

The research project began as a group of Chinese researchers came to Denmark as visiting scholars, which enabled the establishment of a joint project. Discussions and subsequent email correspondence have allowed for an ongoing exchange of ideas. Joint data analysis and authoring of this article have assured a combined Chinese-Danish perspective.

The data consist of interviews and essays. To generate ideas and design the interview guide, a workshop with Danish and Chinese students enrolled in a dual degree program was held in October 2011 on the topic of intercultural communication and culture shock.

Furthermore, in early spring 2012, ten Chinese exchange students, all graduate students, aged 23–28, four males and six females, were asked to respond to a questionnaire in written form/essay style. They typically wrote 1½–2 pages on their experiences in Denmark particularly in relation to their experience of the Danish teaching style, PBL and group work in mixed nationality groups.

It must be taken into account that students were asked to respond to these questions by their Chinese University. Implicitly there can be an urge to display oneself as an apt student, even under new circumstances, and a hesitation to criticize both background and host educational culture and institutions. Still the essays are openhearted touching on both positive and negative experiences and comparisons between Denmark and China.

Finally, during the spring 2012, nine Chinese students from study programs spanning from the Humanities to Natural Sciences, and from graduate and undergraduate programs were interviewed individually. Two of these students had already left Denmark and were interviewed through Skype. All interviewees had been enrolled in a PBL-organized program in Denmark for at least one semester. Four male and five female students, aged 21–25, were interviewed. They were recruited through email contact. The first interview was carried out by one of the authors as a test of the interview guide. The following interviews were carried out by a Danish graduate student. Even though an informal atmosphere was attained in the first interview it was assessed to be an advantage with the following student/student setting. Interviews lasted approximately one hour and were transcribed verbatim by student assistants, both Chinese and non-Chinese, and they were afterward compared with the sound files for precision.

Students accepted that essays and interviews would be used in research. In the following, interviewees and essay-writers are anonymized. The perspectives of Danish students and teachers/supervisors will be included in the next phase of the research project.

Findings

Frequently, non-Western students coming to Western universities find themselves silenced and marginalized, socially and academically (Selvarajah 2006). This has also been the case in PBL settings (Woodward-Kron and Remedios 2007). Institutional norms and routines are first and foremost designed to accommodate domestic students, secondly other Western students (in terms of language, credit systems, forms of exam, etc.). That students experience 'difficult times' when exposed to incomprehensible, often even alienating study environments questioning previously acquired knowledge and learning modes is seldom part of the internationalization rhetoric of national and international politicians and policy-makers. Instead, accounts of 'difficult times' emerge in studies giving voice to international students, especially non-Westerners. However, our findings suggest that the PBL approach does entail 'difficult times' but may also facilitate the inclusion and expression of non-domestic (and non-Western) voices and viewpoints.

The Chinese interviewees all experienced group work (2–6 persons) as part of the project work (typically collaboration over 2–3 months in the semester). Some participated in groups with Danish students, others with other international students. Contrary to reports of lacking contact with domestic students in this case, the group work assured communication between students. The project work demands that students remain together even during conflicts among group members. There are several examples of group members also spending time socializing, e.g. cooking food for each other. However, several students also mention that building relationships with Danish students can be difficult.

Although expecting a different learning environment in Denmark, not all students were aware of the PBL orientation before coming. Whereas the informants' knowledge progression in their respective disciplinary areas was more or less as expected, the intensity of their learning experience is understood as connected to their participation in a project group and having first-hand experience of a problem-oriented approach to studying. Multiple accounts of project processes include the choice of a topic, the formation of a group, and the process of grappling with the transformation of topic interest to problem formulation. Furthermore, essential components of the PBL experience are the process of producing the project report within the confinements set by the problem formulation and the interactions between students in the project groups and between the students and their supervisors. The overall picture is not one of smooth or conflict-free collaboration between group members. Rather, several students describe the difficulties of overcoming cultural, disciplinary, and ideological differences between group members in the attempt to reach consensus and a shared text-product. Particularly, social science students experience the influence of different cultural and political backgrounds on the perspectives of their group members regarding the issues studied. Despite disagreements, however, Chinese perspectives were voiced, defended and finally sometimes integrated in the project:

> The biggest challenge in my project writing was cooperating with the foreign group members who have totally different academic and cultural backgrounds, opinions and working styles. When we thought about our topic for the project, we couldn't agree with each other at all. One member criticized everything... At the very beginning, every member was influenced by the information which they have already known or been familiar with, and thought in their own ways... After our exchange of different opinions through positive communication, we became objective instead of subjective... Finally we found balance among the four of us; we started to put effort to arrive at the same destination (essay).

In a similar vein, several students describe that their perspective on acquired knowledge has changed as a consequence of group discussions of the project content. Having to defend one's point of view or trying to convince others of one's arguments creates a sense of ownership in relation to knowledge which benefits the individual student in the oral project exam:

> meanwhile I also enjoyed the discussion among the group members, different people have different opinions. On one hand, I should learn to respect others' ideas; on the other hand, I need to insist on my own opinion if I am sure it would be great helpful to our project (essay).

In addition to ownership of knowledge and an improved ability to communicate, students also mention the ability to relate critically to the knowledge conveyed to them as a competence, strengthened through project work:

> Actually, our group spent almost half of our project time on trying to formulate a proper problem last semester. Seeking a problem itself is a learning process, and following the problem to conduct further study is a more focused, more critical, and deeper learning (essay).

Improved English language skills and recognition of their disciplinary knowledge from their peers in the project group promote more active and critical classroom participation. In agreement with the PBL approach, concrete problems are addressed in the classroom, and student contributions are encouraged.

Among the informants, there is widespread agreement that criticality is a characteristic of the Western students, not the Chinese. However, based on the observation that critical remarks are not only allowed but also valued by teachers, Chinese students feel more or less compelled to adopt the practice of asking critical questions themselves. When doing this, they try to filter out what they perceive as non-qualified criticism. For example, one informant observed that some of her (Chinese) fellow students had learned how to produce (qualified) critical contributions in the classroom, whereas other informants characterized critical comments made by Danish students as occasionally insubstantial and sometimes even 'ridiculous'. The notion of criticality indicates an important point regarding the informants' propensity to air (or suppress) own opinions in the classroom. Critical participation is not constructed as a 'right' to speak one's mind but rather as a more or less well-developed ability. The informants recognize that they do not form a homogenous group in this regard – some are more advanced than others. Thus, classroom contributions are made on the basis of skill rather than in an attempt to challenge the knowledge of teachers or textbooks.

The students interviewed appreciate the competences that group work entails: strengthened language skills, abilities to communicate their own points of view, and improved understanding of the opinions of their peers. The students appreciate the group as a learning resource, i.e. that a lot of information is available within a group of students sharing an interest in the same topic. The informants also report that they have improved their collaborative skills dramatically. At their home universities, teaching, learning, and examination activities are organized around the individual. In Denmark, they are exposed to the experience of group work, where the informants gradually improve their language skills, gain confidence, and learn the ropes from more experienced peers:

> Yes. I think the Danish guy is really good at it. He has experienced several projects, project work. So there is no problems with him. And it is a Chinese girl and she was an exchange student to [City] University when she did the bachelor degree. Now she is a master student and she is in our group, she had experienced it. So this is much helpful for my group and for me (interview).

Several informants suggest that group work makes an impact on Chinese students because the students have a background in a totally different learning environment. Most informants characterize the learning environment at Chinese universities as individualistic and competitive, which is psychologically demanding but also encourages the students to work harder:

> So it is a kind of competition, and that makes the people and especially the students in China,[. . .] they form a way of competitiveness. One advantage is that the students work

> very hard [. . .], but a disadvantage is that it don't make the student to collaborate with others (interview).

The informants emphasize the easy access to teachers and the quantity of time that students can spend with their teachers/supervisors in the Danish university. Chinese students assess the relaxed and informal interaction between Danish students and teachers as less status-oriented than in China. In several cases, however, the informants report that they miss firmer guidance from their supervisors (cf. Du and Hansen 2005). Some of the informants recognize that direct guidance is withheld for pedagogical reasons, i.e. that supervisors want the students to work independently and make their own decisions. However, in a few cases, the lack of clear response from supervisors causes considerable frustration.

The students candidly account for the types of problems they have experienced as part of the group process. Besides language-related communication problems, they often find themselves in groups comprising multiple nationalities. Thus, they have to cope with a wide range of different accents, at the same time as they have to practice their own English language skills.

Although the Chinese students generally express themselves in appreciative terms regarding PBL and the group work model, they also find themselves in a confusing situation because of their unfamiliarity with the entire study environment and PBL-organized studies. In most cases, students attended introductory courses and social programs for international students. Such initiatives are helpful but do not entirely remove experiences of lack of direction and even frustration.

The data provide important insights into many details causing confusion and difficulties in a foreign learning environment: the behavior of teachers and fellow students, the study materials (and the expectations around them), exam forms, and, importantly, the criteria by which academic performance is measured: what counts as a good academic performance in an unfamiliar and culturally different setting? Academic standards are not culturally neutral but influenced by, among other things, the intellectual history of the national university system and the specific institutional tradition. Thus, the Chinese students must adapt not only to a new set of learning practices but also to different academic standards and values. The informants generally report that the academic content of lectures and project work fits well with the knowledge that they have attained at their home universities. What surprises several informants in relation to PBL is the emphasis on methodology and application of and reflection on theories in project work. The informants experience that considerable effort must be put into what could be termed the meta-level or the reflection level of conducting research.

An important coping resource is the ability to observe and detect differences. The informants appear to be very skilled at pinpointing aspects of the Danish academic milieu which differ from their Chinese home universities:

> I have learned how to gather information better. How to search for information online and read and search information from papers. Because I didn't read a lot of papers before I came here. Then after you search the information, how do you choose the best solution, you don't implement directly, you need to think and compare different information. The first step is to how to gather more information, then second step is how you choose and how to combine this information, to make what you need (interview).

> And also I have learnt something from the PBL, it is like the most important thing in the research is not just to read the conclusion and to memorize the conclusion. It is more important with the methodology and you have to implement it. And how do people design their research process or their framework, rather than you just simply remember or memorize its conclusion. [...] This is something very, very important that I have learnt from here. And also that I have realized that lectures here is not a course you take in China, it is not a hand-by-hand course. You have to think by yourself, and that is called innovation (interview).

The ability to identify and describe differences enables students to actively engage problems that arise due to the informants' lack of familiarity with specific methods, practices, and standards. A particularly telling example is the following where two Chinese students decided to engage the challenge of producing the methodology chapter of the project report:

> Some Danish students said that the most difficult part of the project is the methodology part. At the beginning I was even afraid of writing this hard part, because in Chinese thesis we never have this part. We didn't know anything about the definition of methodology and what should be included, it sounded very abstract and impossible to handle well. I know that in some other groups this part was written by the Danish members who had experience about writing methodology, even for them it would take long time to write. But [name of Chinese student] and I decided to face up with this challenge. In fact, it was not as difficult as we had imagined, after reading many models and a few hours discussion, we wrote it out in one single day, which made other members surprised and satisfied (essay).

The data-set contains multiple examples of students accounting for how they – at least retrospectively – welcome opportunities to perform tasks that they are unfamiliar with, and ill prepared for. Such opportunities provide the students with the chance to improve their abilities:

> I think that the American girl, the first language is English, so for Chinese students it is hard to communicate fluently because her English is perfect. We felt a large pressure, because we just worried that our bad behavior or our bad work would influence to her work so we felt always so bad and studied hard. But at last with communication with her we found out that she is so nice... (interview).

> Because for me it feel really hard to write project in beginning. Not only I need English but academically writing English, oh my god. I felt what I wrote was so stupid and I talked with my group members and I wanted to be better (interview).

Thus, the data-set contains several narratives accounting for encountered problems, which have been overcome and difficult times which have been endured, always with an experience of significant learning as a result.

The coping strategies adopted are to observe and analyze the unexpected and perhaps disturbing phenomena and to endure and/or confront potential negative implications. Such strategies were, for example, applied in the adoption of criticality in classroom participation and in the process of overcoming culturally and politically based conflicts in group work. From a Western point of view, such strategies may involve surprisingly little in terms of action and active resistance (e.g. complaint or protests). However, both interviews and essays reveal that these strategies involve considerable reflective activity in terms of attempts to identify key differences and to make sense of them. Students also report changing behavior based on negative experiences or, oppositely, holding on to a practice identified as successful. For example, an MA level student reports how he now writes an individual project after the experience of a somewhat dysfunctional group collaboration, whereas another student describes how she and her group members finally learned how to respect each other and work toward a shared goal after months of culturally and politically based disagreement. These incidents indicate that the informants do act based on their experience of the unfamiliar learning environment but are generally able to postpone reactions until a more thorough understanding of the phenomenon causing disturbance or frustration has been achieved.

Discussion and conclusion

In agreement with much of the literature in the field, the students participating in this study experienced confusion and frustration. However, this study exposes the *temporary* character of these frustrations due to the fact that the interviewed Chinese students master a set of coping strategies including both attitudinal and cognitive/reflective components, such as curiosity, enthusiasm, and perseverance. In opposition to what is found in some studies, several Chinese students in the sample have had significant contact with domestic students or other international students especially through the project work.

The students feel anxious about how to approach a new learning style and express that they sometimes feel 'stupid', but they seem to work hard at getting their contribution 'right' in the PBL context. Thus, the students demonstrate impressive levels of patience and diligence even if they are probably even more challenged in a PBL context than in other Western study abroad contexts. The Chinese students in this sample are disinclined to give up, and seek to learn and understand.

A possible explanation could be different cultural dispositions for dealing with difficult times – also in learning settings. The PBL learning setting is unfamiliar in a double sense: it shares with Western university settings the emphasis on criticality and independent thinking. Furthermore, it is deeply imbued with institution-specific values and practices connected to PBL and project work. Although being prepared for unfamiliarity in terms of teaching and learning organization may increase the level of acceptance and curiosity toward the PBL experience, the initial phase of practicing group-organized PBL studies is indeed 'a difficult time' for most students. Functioning in an international study environment in which English – spoken with many different accents by both students and teachers – is the working language represents a severe challenge to most of the students. Several students report that their own language difficulties often prevent them from participating as actively in project work as they wish. A further problem is lacking knowledge of different aspects of project work. The informants are also surprised by the free, and by Chinese standards no doubt provocative, way Danish students interact with their teachers, and they are surprised to see that teachers and supervisors seem to appreciate this. Finally, some informants also have mixed feelings regarding the oral project exam due to a combination of unfamiliarity with this exam and insecurity regarding language proficiency.

Despite the many unfamiliar features in the Danish PBL setting, the informants do not seem to question the practices and values of PBL-organized studies in any fundamental way, and they generally engage the entire experience with what might be termed 'pragmatic openness'. They detect differences both in terms of differing academic cultures, and value systems, and of details of academic everyday life. The identified differences motivate the informants to form their own learning agendas to overcome the barriers they sense in relation to participating in group work on equal terms with Danish students. Although the previously acquired learning modes of the interviewed students differed considerably from the ones prevalent at the Danish university, their coping strategies turned out to be quite successful. Once the puzzling PBL universe was understood and the required institutional codes and techniques mastered, the informants were able to have their disciplinary knowledge and specific cultural viewpoints recognized due to the institutional framework, i.e. the student-centered working practices of PBL.

Distilling the essence of Chinese students' learning experience in Denmark is a complex task, and students are not homogenous (neither Chinese nor Danish students), even if some shared features appear. On the one hand, several students report that the experience will affect their future academic life in terms of the way in which they engage research processes and their own academic identities. The PBL experience generally pushes the students toward a more research-oriented approach compared to their earlier experiences. On the other hand, the students generally approach values and practices representing fundamentally differing academic philosophies such as for example, criticality and inquiry into even controversial questions in a pragmatic and almost 'technical' way: producing critical remarks, and forming, and expressing one's own opinion on a given matter is simply an ability to be learned, on par with, for example, the ability to perform well in an oral exam. Thus, the Chinese students seem to recognize that the two different types of learning environment (the PBL-organized Western/Scandinavian milieu and the Chinese) require rather different 'survival techniques'/coping strategies, and that the sooner one is able to acquire the needed competences, the better. Therefore, the stay in Denmark means that their repertoire of study-relevant coping skills is expanded, which enables them to function well both in a Western and a Chinese university context.

To ease the 'difficult times' in the transition to studying in an English-speaking PBL environment it seems that more language-training and even more meta-communication on learning styles and expectations to students will be helpful. It is, however, also clear that students pay the price of global student exchange, through frustration and fear of not achieving in an unknown playing field of learning.

The development of the world today makes it difficult to believe in the usefulness of a fixed curriculum. PBL offers the openness and flexibility to keep students adjusting their search for knowledge and solutions updated and relevant, as it is student and problem-driven. Furthermore, the relatively positive experiences of the Chinese students in this sample are no doubt entailed by the close relationship to both supervisors and other students which is part and parcel of the PBL approach.

References

Bartlett, Tom, and Karin Fischer. 2011. "Chinese Students Prove a Tricky Fit on US Campuses; American Colleges Find the Chinese-Student Boom a Tricky Fit." *The Chronicle of Higher Education* 3: 1–8.

Biggs, John. 1998. "Learning from the Confucian Heritage: So Size Doesn't Matter?" *International Journal of Educational Research* 29 (8): 723–738. doi:10.1016/S0883-0355(98)00060-3.

Brunette, Michelle K., Michel Lariviere, Robert J. Schinke, Xing Xiaoyan, and Pat Pickard. 2011. "Fit to Belong. Activity and Acculturaltion of Chinese Students." *Journal of Sport Behavior* 34 (3): 207–227.

Chalmers, Denise, and Simone Volet. 1997. "Common Misconceptions about Students from South-East Asia Studying in Australia." *Higher Education Research and Development* 16 (1): 87–99. doi:10.1080/0729436970160107.

Chan, Carol K. K., and Nirmala Rao, eds. 2010. "The Paradoxes Revisited: The Chinese Learner in Changing Educational Contexts." In *Revisiting the Chinese Learner: Changing Contexts, Changing Education*, 315–349. Dordrecht: Springer Science and Business Media.

Chen, Rainbow Tsai-Hung, Sue Bennett, and Karl Maton. 2008. "The Adaptation of Chinese International Students to Online Flexible Learning: Two Case Studies." *Distance Education* 29 (3): 307–323. doi:10.1080/01587910802395821.

de Graaff, Erik, and Anette Kolmos, eds. 2007. "History of Problem-Based and Project-Based Learning." In *Management of Change. Implementation of Problem-Based and Project-Based Learning in Engineering*, 1–8. Rotterdam/Taipei: Sense Publishers.

Deng, Zongyi. 2011. "Confucianism, Modernization and Chinese Pedagogy: An Introduction." *Journal of Curriculum Studies* 43 (5): 561–568. doi:10.1080/00220272.2011.617837.

Du, Xiangyun, and Søren Hansen. 2005. "Confronting Cultural Differences." *VEST. A Journal for Science and Technology Studies* 17 (3–4): 61–84.

Hendrickson, Blake, Devan Rosen, and R. Kelly Aune. 2011. "An Analysis of Friendship Networks, Social Connectedness, Homesickness, and Satisfaction Levels of International Students." *International Journal of Intercultural Relations* 35 (3): 281–295. doi:10.1016/j.ijintrel.2010.08.001.

Illeris, Knud. 1981. *Modkvalificeringens pædagogik: problemorientering, deltagerstyring og eksemplarisk indlæring* [The Pedagogy of Counter-Qualification: Problem Orientation, Participant Control, and Example-Based Learning]. Copenhagen: Unge Pædagoger.

Kirby, William C. 2008. "On Chinese, European and American universities." *Daedalus* 137 (3): 139–146. doi:10.1162/daed.2008.137.3.139.

Kolmos, Anette. 1996. "Reflections on Project Work and Problem-Based Learning." *European Journal of Engineering Education* 21 (2): 141–148. doi:10.1080/03043799608923397.

Kvale, S. 1996. *Interviewing*. London: Sage.

Li, Jin. 2003. "U.S. and Chinese Cultural Beliefs about Learning." *Journal of Educational Psychology* 95 (2): 258–267. doi:10.1037/0022-0663.95.2.258.

McMahon, Patrick. 2011. "Chinese Voices: Chinese Learners and Their Experiences of Living and Studying in the United Kingdom." *Journal of Higher Education Policy and Management* 33 (4): 401–414. doi:10.1080/1360080X.2011.585739.

Selvarajah, Christopher. 2006. "Cross-Cultural Study of Asian and European Student Perception. The Need to Understand the Changing Educational Environment in New Zealand." *Cross Cultural Management: An International Journal* 13 (2): 142–155. doi:10.1108/13527600610662320.

Wang, Ting, and Leah Moore. 2007. "Exploring Learning Style Preferences of Chinese Postgraduate Students in Australian Transnational Programs." *International Journal of Pedagogies and Learning* 3 (2): 31–41. doi:10.5172/ijpl.3.2.31.

Woodward-Kron, Robin, and Louisa Remedios. 2007. "Classroom Discourse in Problem-Based Learning Classrooms in the Health Sciences." *Australian Review of Applied Linguistics* 30 (1): 1–18. doi:10.2104/aral0709.

Wu, Zongjie. 2011. "Interpretation, Autonomy, and Transformation: Chinese Pedagogic Discourse in a Cross-Cultural Perspective." *Journal of Curriculum Studies* 43 (5): 569–590. doi:10.1080/00220272.2011.577812.

Zhang, Jing, and Patricia Goodson. 2011. "Acculturation and Psychosocial Adjustment of Chinese International Students: Examining Mediation and Moderation Effects." *International Journal of Intercultural Relations* 35 (5): 614–627. doi:10.1016/j.ijintrel.2010.11.004.

Reframing teaching relationships: from student-centred to subject-centred learning

Julia Hobson and Angus Morrison-Saunders

Student Learning Centre, Murdoch University, Murdoch, Australia; Enivronmental Science, Murdoch University, Murdoch, Australia; School of Environmental Sciences and Development, North West University, Mahikeng, South Africa

At a time when the context of teaching in higher education is difficult for many number of factors such as: reduced funding, changing demographics of students and demands to teach in flexible times and spaces, there are also higher levels of quality control, transparency and accountability over teaching which are exerted by institutions. This paper reframes these demands and difficulties to reclaim the disciplinary expertise of the academic as teacher and following Palmer sees teaching as an entanglement of 'beings': the teachers, the learners and the subject and explores what it means to be a teacher within these relationships. We argue for a relational pedagogy in which embodied teaching is guided by listening for and to the subject. Wishing to be consistent in the paper with its theme, we adopt a subject-centred approach. And since our core subject in this paper is teaching, we necessarily include reflections on teaching experiences.

Introduction

The challenges and transformations in the past 20 years of the university as an institution have been well documented and discussed (Barnett 1992, 2000, 2011). In particular, the financial pressures faced by universities, the competition for funding, the forces of globalisation (Shumar 2004); the changing demographics of academically underprepared students (Wingate 2006; Devlin and O'Shea 2012); the rearrangement of teaching into 'flexible times' in which there seems to be no time at all (Clegg 2010); the use of spaces that are not physical (Savin-Baden 2010) and the emphasis on producing the employable, work-ready graduate (Cooper, Orrell, and Bowden 2010). Plus, the difficulties of large amounts of teaching load being carried by casual staff marginally linked to the institution and to students. Finally, the extended surveillance on academics as teachers in terms of quality control, transparency and accountability have all lead to an experience of teaching in difficult times in higher education (Lupton 2013).

Inspired by Palmer (1998), this paper plots a journey in which we explore and reflect upon our personal experiences of tertiary teaching and address ourselves to the question of: what does it mean to be a teacher? Like Palmer (1998), we view teaching as an entanglement of 'beings': the teachers, the learners and the subject. The key aspect that we wish to highlight in this paper is the notion of the subject as a being. The difference we are drawing between subject-centred learning and learning of a subject is the distinction that: 'The subject-centred classroom is characterised by the fact that the third thing has a presence so real, so vivid, so vocal, that it can hold teacher and students alike accountable for what they say and do' (Palmer 1998, 117). We interpret Palmer's use of the word 'thing' through Latour (2004, 233) as, 'A thing is, in one sense, an object out there and, in another sense, an *issue* very much *in* there, at any rate, a *gathering*... the same word thing designates matters of fact and matters of concern'. So, Palmer's 'third thing' that students and teachers gather around is in and of itself a gathering. Subjects studied, from environmental science to philosophy, cannot be divided into realist hard facts versus subjective interpretations of experience but are always matters of concern, are always imbued with and intertwined as facts-values. The 'third thing' is the world speaking to us. We may hear that voice through the sounding boards of environmental science or philosophy or psychology or politics or engineering: and so hear or respond to different words but the world does speak, which means that by attending to the quality of our listening (Hua 2012) we may find a way to reframe teaching in difficult times. Reframing teaching relationships in higher education as a gathering around a subject opens up an endlessly rich and engaging community of learning for teacher and student alike and reminds us that the fundamental reason for teaching (both of teachers and students) is to engage with the world through the subject studied.

Using frame theory and phenomenology, we shift the boundaries of what it means to be a teacher and exemplify this through personal reflection. But teaching does not occur in isolation from the greater social and political forces surrounding universities and society more generally. A second theme revolves around teaching at universities in difficult times, and how we see that a subject-based approach may be put into practice in current sociopolitical circumstances by actively building community. Thus, the paper moves between personal reflections and a reflexive approach which assumes that '... the beliefs of researchers affect the world that they research' (Fox, Martin, and Green 2007, 182).

Reframing the difficulties

Frame theory assumes that the conceptions and system of conceptions that we use change what we observe and notice. Frames are more than a tool for thinking they are dynamic systems that change both what we think and how we interact with the world and each other. To reframe our conceptual system is to change that dynamic (Jerneck and Olsson 2011).

Part of what a frame does is to determine what is considered to be part of the context and what is left out. In our reframing of the difficulties of teaching in higher education, we shift the frame to include the relationship between and with: students, teachers and the subject, not as an add-on but as central to teaching. To conceptualise pedagogy as relational and to enter into a relationship is to be open to change and attend to the relationship. As McGilchrist (2009, 28) points out when discussing the workings of the human brain:

> The kind of attention we bring to bear on the world changes the nature of the world we attend to, the very nature of the world in which those 'functions' would be carried out, and in which those 'things' would exist. Attention changes *what kind of* a thing comes into being for us: in that way it changes the world.

For example, rather than framing the teaching difficulties that a widening and increasing participation in higher education brings through a 'student deficit' model in which students are asked 'to adapt themselves to the institution and its rules, rather than on the institution and its main players to adapt in response to the fresh perspectives' (Bowl 2001, 157); it is to attend to the changing relationship between subject, student and teacher. In any relationship it is the whole person that is involved, not a segment and so this reframing of teaching brings the whole person into being a teacher.

This reframing also highlights the phenomenological method, which draws together insights into, from and through experience via critical reflection and generates detailed, careful descriptions of everyday 'things' to see them in fresh ways (Goulding 2002, 23). Phenomenology takes the approach of examining subjective and personal human experience with an emphasis on an individual's views, feelings and emotions (Harvey 2009; Lopez and Willis 2004). This is a method that assumes all knowing is interpretation, that interpretation is improved through a circle of open peer inquiry and discussion, that methods of inquiry must take great care over close, attentive observations and that those observations must not be limited by preconceptions as to what should or should not be included. Rigorous scholarship using this method means it is necessary to include even those aspects of teaching such as bodily emotions and intuition which are usually considered to have no place in the classroom.

As the teaching context in higher education expands (geographically, sociologically and politically) so the quality of attention to teaching needs to expand not contract and include more of the person in the teacher. This is not to become the overburdened 'martyr' carrying greater workloads, but to expand the sense of self in relationship with and to others including the subject. It is to redefine the framing of what it means to be a teacher.

Teachers matter. It has been said before and it will be said again; not the teaching but the teacher matters (Fenstermacher and Richardson 2004). Who has not heard the following reflective question at some point in an academic development session of: 'Think of a teacher who influenced your learning style/trajectory/journey?', and listened to a flurry of affectionate and powerful memories of a person who shaped that person's thinking? It is not the 'what' that we remember but the 'who'! We must begin therefore by reframing teaching by reframing ourselves. And to do that is to begin with an autobiography (Campbell, McNamara, and Gilroy 2004).

How did we come to be teachers?

Julia

> I did not set out to be a teacher and after 20 odd years of teaching at university I still have no qualifications as a teacher. Rather, like most of my colleagues, I have a PhD in my subject area (philosophy); have completed many short professional development courses run through the university and had lots and lots of practice on the bodies and minds of 1000s of undergraduate students. I was also lucky to experience inspirational and transformative teaching as an undergraduate from Dr Patsy Hallen, a now retired academic at Murdoch University, whose gentle yet strong insistence on authentic engagement with texts and ideas opened up the life of the mind for me as a young student. A door once opened that can never be closed again and thus I fell in love with thinking about thinking and with the joys and thrills of the subject of philosophy. And

so I took the traditional route of casual tutoring, completing a PhD on the philosophical ramifications of quantum theory as considered through David Bohm's metaphysics of wholeness at the end of which, with children to support, I found a secure job in the offshoot world of academic language and learning, becoming a senior lecturer in learning skills.

At first, I resisted the naming of my work as 'teaching'; I was an academic and taught alongside my research and other duties. I facilitated learning, I created conditions for excellent discussions amongst students, I inducted students into the discourse of academia but I did not name myself a teacher. I might name myself as a tutor or lecturer but not as a teacher, it was only after a long time of wandering around the university that I have come into being, as a teacher. Coming back to my discipline and supervising research students in philosophy and wondering again, 'What is the pedagogy for beholding interconnectedness as a primary reality and not a derived one?'. (Palmer and Zajonc 2010, 77)

Angus

Having grown up spending a large amount of my time outdoors, with family holidays frequently spent busy camping in the wilds of Australia, studying Environmental Science at university seemed like a natural fit. I was an extremely mediocre student, however, barely scraping through with pass marks for most of the technical units. Things changed in my final year when I was exposed to policy, law and decision-making, including what is now my area of speciality: environmental impact assessment (EIA). I discovered a great passion for this more applied aspect of environmental science.

After completing a basic BSc degree, I was employed briefly and casually to undertake some EIA research, which ultimately resulted in my first publication in the field. By this time, I was hooked and signed up for honours research in EIA following a gap year of travel overseas. During my honours year, I also started teaching for the first time as a casual tutor in an environmental policy and law unit. I continued with the tutoring after graduating and whilst working as a full-time EIA consultant. It did not take me long to realise that I did not enjoy the commercial side of EIA much at all, but really enjoyed the university teaching I had been doing and was hungry for more. Consequently, I enrolled in a PhD in EIA, knowing that this qualification was essential for an academic career.

I have always enjoyed the teaching experience but literally 'fell' into this role with no training or preparation whatsoever, relying entirely upon my wits and self-motivation to do as best as I could at it. My formal reflections on teaching began when I taught units in environmental education (EE) – here for the first time I was exposed to academic literature and thinking about the (environmental) learning experience and a body of knowledge that was seeking to make EE as effective as possible. Thus, I embarked on the journey of self-reflection, awareness and evaluation; always seeking to improve my own teaching. It is fair to say that teaching is equally as beguiling a subject to me as is my long-term love of EIA.

Reframing relationships in teaching

Claiming an identity as a teacher in higher education can be difficult, as we note in our stories. Savin-Baden (2008, 145) remarks, '. . . the notion of "being" a teacher in higher education continues to be a problematic and contested space'. Part of this difficulty is the pressure to learn pedagogical theory and practise when expertise lies in a disciplinary area, this throws all academics (apart from those in the discipline of education) back into being a learner '. . . and for some academics the notion of being a learner while being a lecturer is deeply problematic both emotionally and pedagogically' (Savin-Baden 2008, 145). Reframing this difficulty away from expertise in pedagogical theory and onto teachers as whole people who are passionate about their subject of expertise, takes away some of that pressure. It is to widen the frame to include both those dispositions which are usually recognised as part of the characteristics of good teachers such as: '. . . enthusiastic, dedicated, communicated well, were available to help and did so promptly and explained the course requirements clearly' (Devlin and O'Shea 2012, 394) and to include relational qualities. To begin with what it means to be a teacher, is to allow words from the affective realm into teaching accounts, such as those that emerged in our autobiographies: 'beguiling', 'hungry', 'love' and 'gentle'.

Whilst we would agree with Lupton (2013, 161) that:

> The foregrounding of the teacher might seem at odds with the student-centred approach which has dominated the higher education teaching literature over the last 20 years . . . it could be argued that acknowledging the mind-body-spirit of the teacher as a crucial dimension in teaching and learning is integral to a student-centred approach.

We would add that it is the entanglement of both teacher and student in relationship with the subject, the 'great' thing, that is being studied which is at the centre of the classroom. As Palmer (1998, 116) describes it:

> Perhaps, the classroom should be neither teacher-centred nor student-centred but subject-centred. Modelled on the community of truth, this is a classroom in which teacher and students alike are focused on a great thing, a classroom in which the best features of teacher-and student-centred education are merged and transcended by putting not teacher, not student, but subject at the center of our attention.

We would also add that building this 'community of truth' is through relationship with other teachers. Whilst we may begin with autobiography, we must then move to a sharing of those stories as a way to build community. Academics have often faced difficult times and it is possible to trawl through the institutional history of the Western university and point to any number of these times, for example, student riots in Paris did not just happen in 1968 but also in 1229 when academics at the University of Paris went on strike for two years over the deaths of students and to force the declaration of academic freedom (Courtenay, Miethke, and Priest 2000). However, rather than the collective identity that academics have historically drawn on in times of threats; currently, one of the profound difficulties in teaching in higher education is that the range of academic responses is constrained by an 'enhanced individualism' (Shumar 2004). This is an individualism '. . . which involves a loss of autonomy, a lack of self-determination and a culture of audit and excessive accountability' (Campbell, McNamara, and Gilroy 2004, 29). The struggle against the 'enterprise university' begins when we remember that academics and students *are* the university. A university only exists as a relationship between students and faculty. Indeed, Palmer and Zajonc (2010, 25) suggest that community as a concept exists as, 'an ontological reality, an epistemological necessity, a pedagogical asset and an ethical corrective'. This means that academics and students need to 'take back' the institution, to reclaim the *communitas* of the university as their own, to stand against the environment of increasing surveillance and control of teaching in higher education and do so together, not alone.

Barnett (2011, 451) calls on academics to strive for the best possible idea of a university under present conditions to create an 'ecological university' which brings together '...the apparent tension here between authenticity and responsibility, between the inner and the outer callings of the university...that takes seriously both the world's interconnectedness and the university's interconnectedness with the world'. And a good place to begin is by reconstituting the interconnections within the university so that academics move from an individualised account of their teaching to a collective and shared space with a language to talk about teaching that is authentic to them, a language imbued by the disciplinary subject.

Whilst there are, and have been, good reasons for improving teaching quality in higher education, this can be achieved through institutions increasing trust, supporting risk-taking behaviour and acknowledging the courage that it takes to teach (Palmer 1998). This is not to denigrate the importance of understanding and at times applying teaching strategies, but it is to recognise the limitations of such approaches. For example, John Biggs (1999) wrote an extremely useful and richly textured book aimed to '...help university teachers reflect on and improve the quality of their teaching, despite the conditions of class size and diversity that seem to make good teaching more difficult than ever' (x1). Thirteen years later, most academics have incorporated Biggs's teaching strategies of aligned assessment, authentic classroom activities and scaffolding of curriculum into their practice, yet, still struggle with the question of how best to teach in the context of a higher education system now under even greater pressures from constant demands by a multitude of 'stakeholders'. Just as the conceptualisation of students' approach to learning as shallow/deep/strategic (Entwistle and Ramsden 1983) does not encompass the whole of the learning experience; so approaches to teaching as transfer of knowledge or transformation of students does not encompass the full experience of teaching. It leaves out the transformation of the teacher. Palmer (1998, 10) shows that, 'good teaching cannot be reduced to technique; good teaching comes from the identity and integrity of the teacher'.

Reflections on the integrity of the teaching relationship

Julia

> Recently, I was invited to run a day long professional development seminar at another university for tutors on ways to engage their students in critical thinking. As my seminar was on the second day, I decided that I needed to attend the first day to get a sense of the context and culture of the faculty rather than just walk in, do my thing and leave. I did this because teaching for me is about relationship and it is very difficult to form a relationship so quickly. At least having the day before with the participants talking and drinking tea together, gave us a small chance of succeeding in creating a learning moment the next day. I spent quite a lot of time planning the rise and fall of the day: recognizing that there would be the after lunch lull, building in the easy moments at the beginning, scaffolding the interactions within the room so that the participants would have moments of engagement, moments of quiet reflection, moments of taking in (possibly) new ways of thinking about the tasks; moments of modeling and moments to practice new approaches. The day flowed as I had anticipated until after lunch I threw out the planned session and changed to a session with much more space in it because something had happened: thinking had entered the room.

Sometimes when I teach I notice a shift within the attention of the room, not of individuals but a collective shift, and I term this 'thinking entering the room'. I experience this shift as a presence arriving that changes the quality of what we are all doing at that moment – whether it be talking, listening, reading or writing. This is the experience of thinking as a collective act, which intensifies, sharpens and deepens the capacity of each of us to think.

On this day when I saw thinking arrive I let go of the plan, let go of the control and opened the space for participants to synthesis and integrate the material already covered into a lesson plan for their students, and to present these lesson plans to the seminar group. They covered the white boards in that room with brilliant, creative, innovative teaching ideas far beyond anything I had suggested and did this all in one hour. At the end of the session as we were reviewing together what had been created in that room, I found myself moved to tears (which I just managed to hold back) by the generosity of these people. And I remembered what it was about those inspirational moments with Patsy Hallen as an undergraduate and a postgraduate that had changed me: it was love.

Angus

Recently, I conducted a World Cafe with my students on the rich topic of (environmental) decision-making and trade-offs. I had never facilitated a World Cafe before, but had previously thoroughly enjoyed several community-based events at which the technique was used; it was such an amazing energising feeling when passionate discussions occurred spontaneously throughout the room. I wanted to achieve something of the same with my students. It turned out that I was in for a roller coaster of emotions as the World Cafe with my students unfolded and few of my expectations eventuated!

I explained the basic structure for the World Cafe involving small group discussions upon three challenging questions concerning decision-making issues with group changes to occur for each question. I set up the 'cafe' tables with plenty of blank paper and pens to enable furious scribbling, jotting or doodling to take place by anyone and everyone in a group during their discussion (i.e. this had been the experience in community-based World Cafes I had previously attended). I also provided sticky notes to enable each group to capture key ideas from their discussions that would be pasted onto the classroom walls under each discussion question, for whole-of-class deliberation at the very end.

I assigned the membership of the first set of small groups (thereafter the students self-selected groups when it came time to 'move on') so as to break up the regular peer groups that the students formed each week during class. The students all moved to their new groups and I invited them to commence discussions.

The room remained silent! It was everything I could do to stop myself from commanding them to speak. It was agony, and so I left the room for five minutes or so. When I returned each group was engaged in very subdued discussion – there was none of the hubbub I had so vividly enjoyed in the community-based World Cafes. Also there was no scribbling on the paper provided; instead each student was busy writing notes in their own private notebooks. I deliberately did not sit-in or listen-in on the conversations of the groups, as I normally would during small group discussions, as I did not want to impose in any way upon their own thinking and learning and group dynamics. My only communication with them was to invite each group to write up at least one sticky note and to paste this on the classroom wall, prior to them forming new discussion groups and moving onto the next question. It seemed like hard work to get them to write up just one sticky note per group per question – again this was in great contrast to the previous World Cafe experiences where comments proliferated.

While the students were involved in their discussions, I jotted down my observations of the event, noting that it did not seem to working all that well because it was so different from my previous experiences and hence expectations. When I felt that the discussions had probably come to a useful end (intuited from the energy levels in the room) I commenced a whole-of-class discussion.

I was astounded (and relieved!) when several students voluntarily spoke up and said it was one of the best discussions that they had ever had in a classroom and that they really appreciated meeting and talking to other students that they normally would not engage with. They observed that this exposed them to different ideas, and they noted it was far superior to discussions in previous weeks of the semester. They then asked me to share the contents of the sticky notes with them. Up until this point, I had not looked at their content; I had just been disappointed with the small number received.

Reading aloud the sticky notes, I was amazed at the sophisticated, nuanced and extremely well thought-through responses to the discussion questions. I could not have asked for better subject-related content and it exceeded all of my expectations. Perhaps, my excitement in reading out the student responses and sharing my own reaction to them inspired the students. Because all of sudden they had leapt to their feet and were using their mobile phones to photograph all the comments. And then one of them said: 'We could post these on the online Discussions Forum for the external students to share!' I was thrilled needless to say.

What had been, for me, a teaching experiment, for which I had held strong pre-conceived notions of how it 'should' proceed had unfolded in a completely different way, and ultimately surpassed my expectations regarding the learning content and experience. I learnt that teaching must be something that the community of learners owns and shapes for themselves. While I was responsible for the initial skeletal structure and learning content to some extent (i.e. a World Cafe would not work for questions with 'black and white' answers – they must revolve around topics that invite in-depth discussion and multiple 'shades of grey'), I had to relinquish control and let the subject speak for itself and to capture the student's full attention. It took personal courage on my behalf and I had to endure a couple of hours of self-doubt, fear and loathing, but the experience ultimately transcended all expectations.

Reflexivity: reflecting on reflections

As revealed in our previous reflections, neither of us set out to become teachers, but rather somewhat 'fell' into the role. Labelling oneself as a university teacher may superficially evoke the 'duty statement' description of academic teaching responsibilities. A focus on the tasks of teaching is often undertaken in light of the current difficult times being experienced at Australian universities and elsewhere in terms of increasing class sizes, seemingly poorer entry-level education standards, stretched resources, etc. But the nuances of tertiary teaching are so much richer than this functional level of consideration. Through a reflective practice developed over many years we have come to understand the deeper philosophical meanings of 'being as a teacher'.

The unifying experience for both of us has been to learn to listen to and trust our own inner voices. Our students and our subjects communicate with us at a subliminal level that we have learnt to be receptive to and seek out gently. Thus, when thinking enters the room, or students become beguiled and engaged in the subject for themselves, we have learned how to let go of 'control' of the teaching and to enter into the learning experience along with our students.

For us there can be no other way to be effective teachers. The difficult times faced in universities will not be solved by technique-based solutions; notwithstanding the importance of the ongoing conversation between academics that surrounds training and capacity developing events as well as the published literature. Through personal transformation and self-awareness, and through the journey each of us has inadvertently experienced in our own ways, we know that any apparent obstacles to tertiary teaching can be overcome, together. Whilst we work in different areas of the university we have connected to each other (and to others) through our reframing of teaching as being.

We listen to our being in order to teach. When we are listeners as teachers then there are ways to work with qualities of listening. As teachers, we listen to our students to hear what they think, what they understand and the meanings they construct (Dewey 1933). We also listen for the moments of understanding of students and the usual form of this listening at university is through assignments and exams. However, another form of listening is when we listen with our students to what the subject is saying to us. And then:

> When the great thing speaks for itself, teachers and students are more likely to come into a genuine learning community, a community that does not collapse into the egos of students or teachers but knows itself accountable to the subject at its core. (Palmer 1998, 118)

We are advocating that as teachers, one of the most effective things we can do is simply bring our attention onto the subject at hand, and enable our students to join us in this mutual inquiry. In this manner, teacher and student collectively share in the learning process in a charged atmosphere during which thinking can enter the room. We are also attuned to the power differential that must exist between a teacher and their students, but through our careful listening and as the quote from Palmer above indicates, taking a subject-centred approach is a gentle and effective way to manage power differences. We are able to discern the need to provide guidance or a firm hand, for example, when marking assessments in order to uphold the minimum academic expectations laid out in our unit materials, while at the same time aiming to provide opportunity for our students to enter freely and deeply into their own relationship with our shared subject.

One of the ways that we have noticed the quality of attention extending in our teaching is when we include bodily and emotional awareness. Listening for the teaching moments with hearts and bodies, paying careful attention to the tingles of skin, the jolts of nerves, the catches in throat, the visceral feelings in the belly (when things are going badly) and the irrepressible urge to smile (when things are going well), has been a reliable guide for us in our years of teaching. When we follow a question with students, when we sit with a question in silence; when we ask of each other what do not we know, then inner attention to bodily tuning is most intense. When we feel the atmosphere of the room thicken we know a need for gentle, slow movements; yet sometimes we step clumsily into a moment and the learning scatters and the students freeze. But in all this it is our trust in ourselves and in our small community of like-minded teachers that gives us the courage to know what it is to be a good teacher, it is programmed into our very being. So it is as though we keep 'relearning' for ourselves at a conscious level what it means to be a good teacher. But that relearning process only has space/opportunity to emerge when we ourselves are tuned into the emotional and physical sensations arising from the teaching experience; in short, behaving like a lover.

We are not claiming particular expertise as teachers, but rather expressing a relational pedagogy. After years of pursuing 'method' or 'techniques' for effective teaching, it is somewhat ironic to realise that the magic lies within us, our students and our subject all along. As Palmer (1998, 2) notes: 'we teach who we are' or put even more simply: teaching is being. And at the intimate relationship level of teacher, subject and student, in the centre of teaching and learning lives love.

References

Barnett, R. 1992. *Improving Higher Education: Total Quality Care.* Bristol: Open University Press.

Barnett, R. 2000. *Realizing the University in an Age of Supercomplexity.* Bristol: Open University Press.

Barnett, R. 2011. "The Coming of the Ecological University." *Oxford Review of Education* 37 (4): 439–455. doi:10.1080/03054985.2011.595550.

Biggs, J. 1999. *Teaching for Quality Learning at University.* Buckingham: The Society for Research into Higher Education.

Bowl, M. 2001. "Experiencing the Barriers: Non-traditional Students Entering Higher Education." *Research Papers in Education* 16 (2): 141–160. doi:10.1080/02671520110037410.

Campbell, A., O. McNamara, and P. Gilroy. 2004. *Practitioner Research and Professional Development in Education*, 28–48. London: Paul Chapman.

Clegg, S. 2010. "Time Future- the Dominant Discourse of Higher Education." *Time Society* 19 (3): 345. doi:10.1177/0961463X10381528.

Cooper, L., J. Orrell, and M. Bowden. 2010. *Work Integrated Learning: A Guide to Effective Practice.* London: Routledge.

Courtenay, W. J., J. Miethke, and D. Priest, eds. 2000. *Universities and Schooling in Medieval Society.* Leiden: Brill.

Devlin, M., and H. O'Shea. 2012. "Effective University Teaching: Views of Australian University Students from Low Socio-Economic Status Backgrounds." *Teaching in Higher Education* 17 (4): 385–397. doi:10.1080/13562517.2011.641006.

Dewey, J. 1933. *How We Think: A Restatement of the Relation of Reflective Thinking on the Educative Practice.* Lexington, MA: Heath.

Entwistle, N. J., and P. Ramsden. 1983. *Understanding Student Learning*. London: Croom Helm.

Fenstermacher, G., and V. Richardson. 2004. "An Inquiry into the Moral Dimensions of Teaching." In *Learning to Read Critically in Teaching and Learning*, edited by L. Poulson and M. Wallace, 110–127. London: Sage.

Fox, M., P. Martin, and G. Green. 2007. *Doing Practitioner Research: Developing the Practitioner Researcher*, 180–195. London: Sage.

Goulding, C. 2002. *Grounded Theory: A Practical Guide for Management, Business and Market Researchers*, 9–37. London: Sage.

Harvey, M. 2009. "Drama, Talk, and Emotion: Omitted Aspects of Public Participation." *Science, Technology and Human Values*, 34 (2): 139–161. doi:10.1177/0162243907309632.

Hua, Z. 2012. "Turning to the Pedagogy of Listening." *Complicity: An International Journal of Complexity and Education* 9 (1): 57–74.

Jerneck, A., and L. Olsson. 2011. "Breaking Out of Sustainability Impasses: How to Apply Frame Analysis, Reframing and Transition Theory to Global Health Challenges." *Environmental Innovation and Societal Transitions* 1: 255–271. doi:10.1016/j.eist.2011.10.005.

Latour, B. 2004. "Why Has Critique Run Out of Steam? From Matters of Fact to Matters of Concern." *Critical Inquiry* 30 (2): 225–248. doi:10.1086/421123.

Lopez, K., and D. Willis. 2004. "Descriptive versus Interpretive Phenomenology: Their Contributions to Nursing Knowledge." *Qualitative Health Research* 14 (5): 726–735. doi:10.1177/1049732304263638.

Lupton, M. 2013. "Reclaiming the Art of Teaching." *Teaching in Higher Education* 18 (2): 156–166. doi:10.1080/13562517.2012.694098.

McGilchrist, I. 2009. *The Master and His Emissary: The Divided Brain and the Making of the Modern World.* London: Yale University Press.

Palmer, P. 1998. *The Courage to Teach.* San Francisco, CA: Jossey-Bass.

Palmer, P., and A. Zajonc. 2010. *The Heart of Higher Education.* San Francisco, CA: Jossey-Bass.

Savin-Baden, M. 2008. *Learning Spaces: Creating Opportunities for Knowledge Creation in Academic Life.* New York: Open University Press.

Savin-Baden, M. 2010. "Changelings and Shape Shifters? Identity Play and Pedagogical Positioning of Staff in Immersive Virtual Worlds." *London Review of Education* 8 (1): 25–38. doi:10.1080/14748460903557662.

Shumar, W. 2004. "Global Pressures, Local Reactions: Higher Education and Neo-liberal Economic Policies." *International Journal of Qualitative Studies in Education* 17 (6): 823–839. doi:10.1080/0951839042000256475.

Wingate, U. 2006. "Doing Away with 'Study Skills'." *Teaching in Higher Education* 11 (4): 457–469. doi:10.1080/13562510600874268.

A heuristic for analysing and teaching literature dealing with the challenges of social justice

Priya Narismulu

English Studies in the School of Arts, University of KwaZulu-Natal, Durban, South Africa

Transformation involves rethinking values and ways of seeing and acting, particularly as time stress compounds legacies of oppression and systematic underdevelopment in many postcolonial countries. These are exacerbated by structural challenges, as many societies are undergoing national, democratic, urban, race, class and gender revolutions simultaneously. All these challenges are aggravated by globalised systems of financial domination and mismanagement. Given these contexts, citizens and intellectuals in developing societies need more effective tools for analysing and deconstructing their challenges, and for the formidable tasks of reconstruction. Overhauling old values and systems to address pivotal challenges such as education and social justice requires metacognitive skills. Developing heuristics to enable integrated thinking, particularly in the arts (in this case English literary studies), helps students use disciplinary building blocks to address contextual challenges. This synthesising strategy is used to overcome histories of systemic violence, disempowerment, neglect, division, marginalisation and silencing in society and education.

Introduction: placing value

> The Committee found that the transformation of what is taught and learnt in institutions constitutes one of the most difficult challenges this sector is facing [and recommends that universities] assess [their curricula for]...appropriateness and relevance in terms of the social, ethical, political and technical skills and competencies....in the context of post-apartheid South Africa,...Africa and the world. (Ministerial Committee on Transformation and Social Cohesion and the Elimination of Discrimination in Public Higher Education, referenced Department of Education 2008, 21)

Teaching in higher education is considered central to social and educational transformation (e.g. Mezirow 1997), the more so in societies tackling oppression. Consonant with the needs of a society, continent and world undergoing profound shifts, the transformation of higher education requires a fundamental shift in values. The question of where value is placed is pivotal to social and educational transformation, for it is a foundational determinant of whether transformation will occur. In education systems, the placement of value helps clarify whether transformation can have any social, epistemic, ontological or structural dimensions (Kincheloe 2003; Clegg 2011). It is also central, if implicit, in the constitution or analysis of any human system. And it is inherent in the development of an ethos of social justice among individuals, groups, institutions, communities and societies attempting to tackle the various forms of oppression (structural, coercive, ideological, cultural, national or global) that have hijacked most lives and futures.

High levels of metacognitive, analytical, syncretic and reconstructive skills are necessary to understand or serve any society undergoing multiple shifts. Responding to various educational and social justice challenges, this article considers how a heuristic tool may help university students develop transformative skills and practices that counter colonial/apartheid/patriarchal/class ontologies and epistemologies to navigate the conjunctural challenges of time, place, race, gender, class, nation, language and culture.

Place and the value of social justice

Social justice is central to the transformation of countries like South Africa, which have experienced colonialism or elite/minority domination. Social justice is known as diversity in western societies, which generally have inverse proportions of oppressed and empowered citizens to societies that were colonised (e.g. South Africa experienced an arduous form of settler colonialism, i.e. apartheid). Postcolonial societies struggle to tackle the intellectual and educational hegemonies that have prevailed, partly because of basic challenges with the validity of ontologies and concepts that have been adopted uncritically.

Social justice and education are both, in profound ways, about the placement of value, which is a challenge in any postcolonial state. This is exacerbated by the power of the clashing value systems that generated global financial and ecological mismanagement. Transformative conceptions about what is valued necessarily inform educational and social justice projects, and raise questions about how normative intellectual and academic values are constituted, sustained or overhauled. Challenging the hegemonic values that have dominated our lives and discourses is integral to transforming the systems they have supported. In higher education, some of this may be done by developing a range of metacognitive skills equal to these tasks.

Challenging assumptions about the assignment of value is central to tackling the chauvinisms and bigotry that are still rife in our society and the world. Bigotry is rooted in pride and ignorance, which in turn are rooted in fear, all of which are antithetical to what universities should be. That our supposedly postcolonial public universities remain challenged by various forms of old and new prejudices (Department of Education 2008; Soudien 2010; Nyamnjoh 2012) suggests the scale of transformation required. Far from reproducing various forms of chauvinism and entertaining bigotry, universities need to actively enable the development of cultures of social justice.

Social justice represents an important challenge to the higher education sector. If taken seriously, responses to this challenge could generate growth well beyond the unrepresentative and limited individual and group subject positions, histories and interests, to which too many intellectuals imagine themselves tied. The problem is not just the hegemony of old forms of identity and power, but also that many intellectuals and managers who subscribe to transformation fail to advance it in their analyses and actions.

The diversity of our society and world compels recognition of the complexity and inter-relatedness of our identities as individuals, communities, societies and world citizens. While the challenge of social justice is urgent and overdue, scientific research has consistently supported the Darwinian hypothesis that the complex diversity to be found in each individual's identity issues from surprisingly unified sources (e.g. Cann, Stoneking, and Wilson 1987; Cavalli-Sforza, Menozzi, and Piazza 1994), despite the history of chauvinistically inspired constructions of difference. There is reason to be concerned about the quality of thinking that occurs at all levels of South African society. Subcultures of extreme risk-taking, denialism, magical thinking, defensiveness, immaturity, unbridled aggression and an absence of self-reflection are observable as much among intellectuals as anyone else. But the Humanities (where I am located) are meant to be central to the development of critical thinking skills, without which even the most technologically advanced societies are seen to flounder (e.g. as observed in the widespread use of public funds to bail out bankrupt corporations). Clearly, besides being skilled at analysis and deconstruction, intellectuals in transforming societies need effective tools for integrated thinking, to advance on the complex processes of reconstruction that are necessary (Narismulu 1999).

'Across the [African] continent higher education is recognized as a key force for modernization and development' (Teferra and Altbach 2004, 21). This has been undermined by the World Bank's neo-imperial conceptions and determinations for African universities (Mamdani 2007), and compounds the 'epistemological imperialism' (Nyamnjoh 2012, 146) that exists this late in the 'postcolonial' history of the continent. Given that most of our universities are publicly funded makes them accountable for questioning the knowledge they produce, for generating more effective and empowering forms of knowledge and for taking responsibility for the larger social, ecological and epistemological contexts (Narismulu 2009b). Reproducing irresponsible attitudes and values in such contexts reveals a misunderstanding even of the larger economic and ecological crises that beset the world, and which already devastate our vulnerable continent. Identifying, challenging and transforming dysfunctional or bankrupt values, systems and disciplinary/discursive hegemonies to meet the needs of social justice and transformation requires a range of metacognitive, conjunctural and intersectional skills.

Complex conjunctures: accelerated time and simultaneous revolutions

It has long been recognised that people across the world are experiencing intensifying problems of time stress (Clegg 2010). Compounding this crisis is what Guha (2009) identifies as the challenge that postcolonial societies are undergoing multiple revolutions, five in the case of South Africa. Indeed, the national, democratic, race, gender, class and urban shifts comprise not five but six simultaneous revolutions. Such complexities are aggravated by the uncritical (sometimes unconscious) imposition of neo-imperial logics, objectives, time-frames and enterprises. The question of value is vital here (not least because of ambivalence or resistance to one or other revolution by leaders, never mind reactionaries).

The concept of multiple revolutions is a useful frame for individuals and groups to understand and engage effectively with the historical and ongoing challenges of the conjuncture. Time-stress, multiple revolutions and neo-imperial agendas compound the levels of disorientation identified as our postcolonial predicament (Fanon 1963; Cabral 1979), and signal the need for greater clarity and reflection (Clegg 2010) that we may understand and honour all our subjectivities as African, postcolonial and world citizens (Mama 1995). This will enable people to address the confused choices being made by individuals, leaders, institutions and communities. (At the state level, this clarifies a number of contradictions in the 'new' South Africa, e.g. exorbitant arms deals when South Africa has no enemies, assumption of responsibility for odious apartheid debt and HIV/AIDS denialism.)

Living in what remains one of the most divided societies in the world (by any measure, not least the Gini) suggests that the most effective response to the historical, spatial and conjunctural challenges is to develop more integrated ways of understanding and dealing with our realities. Such a strategy tackles the fundamental problem that stymies the supposedly post-apartheid society: the profound devaluation of the humanity of all, whether oppressed or privileged by apartheid, class or gender. The scale of this crisis is evident in the violence found at all levels: inter- and intra-gender/race/class/generation/person/family/community. Awareness that we are undergoing multiple revolutions helps rescue interest groups from competing for scarce resources when cooperation is overdue, or the future is mortgaged.

My own intellectual locations help me recognise the possibilities offered by teaching (and scholarship) to address challenges of intellectuals and the creative arts, and I have focused on the oral and written literature of political, gender, race, class and generational struggles for social justice. Under apartheid having aspired to an intellectual life as a way of dealing with a racist, sexist and elitist world, it was and is still outrageous to find academics replicating the bigotry of the ignorant, unprincipled or emotionally deficient. Many intellectual judgements continue reflect little more than narrow class, race, gender and other interests. Analysis is not just a tool to serve the tastes and judgements of elites, the better to maintain power and privileges (Bourdieu 1984).

These conjunctures challenge publicly funded intellectuals working in publicly funded institutions about the extent to which their teaching or research engages questions of transformation and social justice. Given the scale of the educational, national and global crises, these cannot be neglected or addressed only as a matter of taste (e.g. feminist analyses that omit or marginalise the impact of race and class, in South Africa of all places). Understanding our location in the midst of multiple revolutions alerts academics to the urgent need for developing integrated ways of reading and responding to our complex local–national–global conjunctures, beyond sectarian approaches that say more about whom one is rather than what one is attempting to study or teach. The concept also helps explain why disciplinary and other narrow approaches to deal with challenges like gender violence, tuberculosis or HIV/AIDS have not had much efficacy.

Metacognitive tools to serve complex conjunctures

> theorising agency has a political importance as well as a theoretical relevance .... To act we need to recognise ourselves as agents with the potential for collective agency .... [to] influence the shape of higher education. (Clegg 2005, 160)

Cognitive maturity is central to systems intelligence, and goes beyond the differences of identity, ideology and self-interest, which is where most transformation projects are stymied. Given the scale and clear-cut challenges of our society and world, much of what appears to be ideological differences are actually foreclosed by the cognitive limitations of those in power. Neither have they benefitted as much as many imagine. Systems of inordinate privilege such as apartheid, patriarchy and neo-imperialism are reprehensible enough, without the legacy of cognitive underdevelopment they bequeath their beneficiaries (and those who entertain their hegemony). This effect is apparent throughout higher education in South Africa, as well as in the world financial and ecological systems (both in a state of collapse). Elites (and their adherents) need to unlearn their privileges as their loss (Spivak 1990). That requires awareness and the capacity to reflect critically, which Coulson and Harvey (2013, 1) argue is 'associated with the higher order cognitive processes of self-regulation and metacognition'.

Developing effective teaching and learning (and the reflexive scholarship required) is central to any academic transformation project. Academics need deep understandings of the systems in which we function, to develop curricula and epistemologies that open up and address the dynamic networks of local, regional and global inter-relationships. Transformation depends upon how each person, discipline, school, faculty, college, university, education system and society engages with the challenges and opportunities in the conjuncture. This requires resilience, vision, agency, innovation and leadership, and is predicated upon taking responsibility for improving micro- and macrocosms. Agency is rooted in cognitive maturity, which includes depth and breadth of vision, judgement, clarity, conceptual thinking, planning, ethics, decision-making, engaging with established social norms and anticipating the consequences of decisions and actions, to develop more effective principles and practices, as well as the capacity to address systemic challenges. This resonates with Margaret Archer's (2012) findings that people's capacity for reflexivity increases relative to the impact of structural and cultural morphogenesis (7). Pointing out that 'for the first time in human history the imperative to be reflexive is becoming categorical for all' (1), Archer identifies 'the concurrence of morphogenesis in the realms of structure, culture and agency' (4), for '[t]ogether they "make history"' (5).

For students to be encouraged to work beyond the circumscribed (and often hegemonic) constructs of the mass media and other elites, academics, curricula and educational systems need to transform. Many of our public universities are making attempts to tackle the challenges but do not yet have enough will, capacity or resources (Department of Education 2008; Cross 2004). Part of the solution may lie in paradigm shifts, along the lines of critical transformative approaches (e.g. Starfield 1996 in Cross 2004); or more integrated systems, perhaps along the lines of systems intelligence (Hämäläinen and Saarinen 2004), which could include developing emotional, social and spiritual intelligence, through the taking of responsibility for transforming entire systems.

Diversity is not the problem. Our diverse classrooms offer valuable opportunities for advancing the development of dialogue; concern for other's viewpoints, rights and welfare; a democratic ethos and skills; and the development of honesty, tolerance and trust, as argued by Pamela Barnett (2011), who references a significant range of research studies indicating that 'substantive diversity experiences develop cognitive and social capacities' (672). Barnett cites studies showing that cognitive development improves when students engage in problem-solving tasks with peers, particularly in heterogeneous groups, which generate greater gains in integrative complexity.

Given the slow pace of curriculum and pedagogical transformation, it is important to offer students (and young academics) strategies against the alienation, apathy, opportunism and chaos, to make them aware that they can and should change the world, or at least try to make a difference. Reflexivity, agency, effective analyses, and transformation require metacognitive skills and approaches to problem solving. Students learn to manage their thinking processes more effectively, to judge when and how it is necessary to undertake particular tasks, and to check that they are managing such tasks effectively. Basic metacognitive strategies include planning, monitoring and evaluating thinking processes, and are particularly valuable in fields that focus on subjective expression, like literature and all the arts. Metacognitive approaches to learning tend to focus on:

- the values, purposes, goals, objectives, and most effective tools of learning,
- how to develop better ways of understanding the world, texts and other people,
- how to link new information to existing knowledge, and
- how to select the most effective thinking and learning strategies (e.g. Vrugt and Oort 2008)

Such strategies can serve a transformational agenda of teaching and learning. I use the following questions in my lectures in English literary studies to help develop the metacognitive approaches of my students (and myself):

- What is the significance and purpose of the section/texts/theoretical approaches?
- Which ideas and concepts help make sense of each text/section?
- What viewpoints are presented and how effectively do writers/oral performers use language and art to transmit these?
- What are the authors' views, feelings, values, assumptions and goals (as relevant), and how do these impact on the texts?
- What challenges are the authors trying to address?
- How does studying these characters, themes, genres, and texts (primary and secondary) affect your/others' views of the world?
- How will the content knowledge and representation skills be useful to you/others?

Such questions are raised to enable students monitor and evaluate their own thinking processes, so that they learn to address more complex challenges with greater skills and confidence. University students, in particular, need to be empowered and challenged (Barnett 2011) to tackle current and future challenges.

Using a heuristic to navigate complex conjunctures

> Through ingenuity, liabilities inherited from the past can be converted into assets and currency for renewal. Commitment to intellectual revival and development is needed to transcend the formerly crippling spatial isolation. (Nkomo, Swartz, and Maja 2006, 13)

As valuable as metacognitive strategies are for addressing academic and pedagogical challenges, an increasingly complicated and diverse world (e.g. see Huber and Hutchings 2005) requires taking responsibility for more integrated approaches to social, political and cultural analyses. Given our received and endemic problems with honouring social justice and equitable representation, not least in our university systems, advancing more integrated ways of seeing our world and ourselves is crucial. Pedagogies for integrative learning draw on metacognitive thinking, and tend to be constructivist:

> Students are engaged in 'making meaning'...activating a dynamic process of question posing, problem posing, decision making, higher-order critical thinking and reflexivity. A set of core capacities emerge...
>
> - asking meaningful questions about complex issues and problems,
> - locating multiple sources of knowledge, information and perspectives,
> - comparing and contrasting them to reveal patterns and connections,
> - acknowledging and negotiating their contradictions,
> - creating an integrative framework and a more holistic understanding,
> - understanding issues and positions contextually,
> - being able to use information by integrating into their existing knowledge and adapting it so that it can be used in other situations (Klein 2005, 3 cited by Jackson 2009, 8).

Such pedagogies help counter the divisive and alienating apartheid/neo-imperialist/patriarchal discourses and logics that are so insidious, they undermine even the thinking of people who consider themselves well integrated in society.

I have developed a heuristic in response to the deeply felt analytical, pedagogical and social needs for what Michael Apple (2008) calls 'synthesizing strategies', to address neo/colonial dislocation and the complexities of multiple revolutions. The word heuristic comes from the Greek word for 'find' or 'discover', and refers to experience-based techniques that help in learning, discovery and problem solving; all central to our challenges with subject positions, history and education. Overcoming histories of vested interests and blind spots (Narismulu 1998, 2000, 2003), neo-imperialism (Narismulu 2009b), and widespread confusion about identities and interests requires a range of personal, social, interpretive, analytical, communication, argument-construction and writing skills.

The aim of the heuristic is to allow for dialogue across inherited wastelands of difference. The heuristic scaffolds the power of literary art forms that counter our histories of fragmentation and silencing by offering readers ways of navigating a range of conjunctures (Narismulu 2011). The heuristic also enables students to experience, analyse and articulate the richness of our context beyond the received/imposed subject positions and the limitations of some powerful literary, social and intellectual discourses (for a deconstruction of these see, e.g. Narismulu 1998, 2000). My purpose is to teach that instead of being vexatious problems to be managed, social differences can be very productive, if we learn to understand diversity in all its variety and complexity. Having skilful guides in the form of a number of lively literary texts makes this a very engaging task (as discussed in Narismulu 2011).

While responding to the need for crosscutting analyses, the heuristic is also used to respond to the complication that 'the litany of "gender–class–race" is often not accompanied by an intersectional analysis that actually is, either theoretically or methodologically' (Denis 2008, 685). As Ann Denis explains, intersectional analysis involves taking into account three or more variables concurrently (685). Earlier in the article she points out that:

> Intersectional analysis involves the concurrent analyses of multiple, intersecting (and interacting) sources of subordination/oppression and is based on the premise that the impact of a particular source of subordination may vary, depending on its combination with other potential sources of subordination (or of relative privilege). (Denis 2008, 677)[1]

The heuristic I have developed for under- and postgraduate teaching over the past decade does this while answering the need for metacognitive skills, and I refer to it during my illustrative analyses in lectures. It has been necessary to develop different forms of the heuristic depending on the level of the module and the genre/s being taught. I initially adapted a heuristic developed for the purposes of my own research to assist students, many of whom are materially very close to the texts I teach, yet, culturally estranged (again the pernicious legacy of apartheid, in toxic combination with class insecurities). This has helped students construct more integrated responses to the challenges of analysing a narrative/poem/drama/secondary text at the same time as they take account of the conjunctural themes of place, race, gender, class, nation, and so on (Narismulu 2009a).

The heuristic that undergraduate students find at the end of the Introductory Notes in their Workbooks does not announce itself as such (because the goal is not to intimidate, but develop confident and capable young intellectuals). It is offered as a tool that students may use to develop their analytical skills. This is what the heuristic looks like in one of the five sections I have taught in English Studies (from first year to coursework MA level). It is from a first year introduction to the South/African short story (see Narismulu 2011). The references to form are in italics to indicate how discipline-specific elements are integrated into the analytical scheme.

Depending on which story you are examining, select appropriate options to critically analyse how and why each writer:

- follows/explores/challenges the apartheid/patriarchal/capitalist/ethnocentric/ etc. logics and stereotypes in the construction, interactions and conflicts of the *characters*,
- follows/explores/challenges the apartheid/patriarchal/capitalist/ethnocentric logics and stereotypes in the construction of the *narrator*,
- creates characters/narrator that express/deviate from (one of a range of) African women/men's subject positions, subjectivities (points of view, values, ideologies) and discourses that have been coded/silenced/dominant,
- sets up the *plot* by contesting apartheid/patriarchal/capitalist/ethnocentric logics/discourses/stereotypes of power,
- develops *themes* that engage/critique apartheid/patriarchal/capitalist/ethnocentric conceptions of power,

- uses *forms and elements of style* influenced by old/alternative/new ways of thinking about gender/race/class/nationality/age/ethnicity, *etc.*,
- raises old/alternative/new questions, challenges and solutions,
- explores/articulates/mediates/challenges liberatory, generative and creative aspects of African experience, e.g. the *role* of the oral story teller, at the centre of communal life, as an educator, healer, historian or social conscience; or by drawing on the oral tradition and its resources to strengthen/restructure/mute certain subject positions (English 102 Short Stories: Introductory Notes: Conceptual Framework:4).

Part of the reason I developed the heuristic for students is that there is little time in lectures to focus on metacognitive skills, as the general expectation in English Studies is that a large number of texts need to be covered. The heuristic also helps students overcome some of the skills deficits endemic to our educational systems. I try to integrate these academic development processes into my lectures and tutorial worksheets, at the same time offering students tools to deal with the chauvinisms that inform our personal, public, academic, national and global discourses (Narismulu 2011). By yoking these together, students may learn to read the various social and educational deficits as issuing from similar sources of oppression. This can help students focus their imaginative and analytical resources on overcoming shared challenges to find solutions. It is clear from many years of taking lectures, tutorial classes and marking that most of our students are able to grasp the complexities of what they experience even if they have been unable to articulate this, because they are not accustomed to public analyses of discrimination or because they have been or have felt silenced.

The heuristic tries to help students engage with the reality of historical and social differences and the need for social justice and dialogue. It seeks to develop thinking that takes account of, as well as transcends, conceptual prisons (Spivak 1990). In South Africa, this means various intersecting conceptual prisons (as described earlier). The heuristic enables students to focus on individual variables, on the interrelatedness or tensions between particular variables, and develop comprehensive overviews. It allows for the transfer of knowledge, skills and insights from areas more accessible to an individual student (owing to her/his race/class/gender/ethnic/national etc. identity) to areas that may be less accessible, so that each individual or group may go beyond habitual points of view to overcome perceptual limitations and inherited/learned biases. It encourages a student to ask questions in and across all areas and not just in some areas, so that she/he is not trapped in a particular subject position (a challenge that stumps virtually everyone, even today).

Just as the ability to decode social texts is central to anyone's capacity to survive in the world, the capacity to engage skilfully with a range of discourses and texts is central to young intellectuals' capacity to function effectively and make progress. The challenges of producing, reproducing and recontextualizing knowledge (Bernstein 1996, cited in Apple 2008) are all the more difficult in postcolonial societies. An integrated analytical method for tackling core knowledge (of the self, social identities, prescribed texts and creativity) may strengthen young intellectuals' capacities to seek and generate solutions in other areas of their lives and work.

What informs the ongoing process of developing, teaching and researching the heuristic (Narismulu 2009a) is a sense of the students as emerging intellectuals (and prospective civil servants, entrepreneurs and leaders) who need to develop their own independent frameworks of analysis. I believe this can happen if we address three challenges that have proven to be surprisingly elusive to most people, never mind, intellectuals: making sense of where we are (space-time location), who we are (subjectivity), and what is to be done (agency). Clearly, this is not only a matter of cognitive skills, as important as they are, but of systematically taking account of our historical and conjunctural challenges, and not pretending they do not exist (more escapism, endemic in the arts, and more so in English Studies, notwithstanding the long postcolonial period). This, then, is a reflexive response to the challenge of representing and engaging our complex society and world, that are growing not less but more diverse (part of which is a function of our increasing sensitivity). In other societies and disciplines there is increasing awareness of the need for integrated analyses (e.g. Hämäläinen and Saarinen 2004; Jackson 2009), and for creating tools that combine social and textual analyses. In our context, this is of particular value:

> for the development of a vibrant continental intellectual culture, which draws on the diverse perspectives of the widest possible range of social groups and which can produce both the knower and the knowledge that Africa needs to think her way out of crises and move forward into the twenty-first century. (Mama 2006, 29)

Agency is not just a value of the task; engaging in the task also helps scaffold and develop the agency (i.e. the skills, thinking and actions) of the learning subject.

Conclusion: towards ontological and epistemological integration

> To understand myself better, I need to find others who are living this struggle to determine their work as teachers fighting for social justice and equity. (Ross 2007, 9–11)

The placement of value is central to the development of social justice and intellectual skills, particularly in the context of disabusing students of unwittingly bigoted or neo-imperial antagonisms to the values of justice and inclusivity. The question of values also informs curriculum development, pedagogical approaches and scholarship.

The methods used in the teaching contribute to what I believe are the important transformative tasks of each person and each publicly funded intellectual, and which begin with operationalizing the challenge of finding one's voice in all its fullness and being empowered by it (Greene 2000). By drawing on a range of relevant literary texts, students learn to name the obstacles that prevent the achievement of their own and others' full humanity (Freire 1973), and how to deal with these. The effects could be life changing (Grumet 1980), which may encourage some students to try to change (transform) the world (Freire 2004). This is not idealistic. In fact, it is driven by some serious limitations. As I find myself saying to each class group:

> I am trying to prepare you to solve problems that previous generations, including mine, have failed to address, and some of which my generation has caused. You need to take advantage of every opportunity to prepare to solve these problems and to tackle other exciting challenges that I cannot anticipate, let alone imagine.

The challenges facing our society, continent and world require 'a much higher level of intellectual, strategic and creative capacity' (Mama 2006, 28). As an academic, scholar and citizen in a society struggling to heal and transform itself, I am interested in how heuristics and metacognitive skills advance the development of critical, creative and democratic responses to local, national, regional, continental and global challenges. Such instruments strengthen the practices of teaching and learning, increasing the contribution and value of the arts, humanities, social sciences and higher education.

Note

1. The intersectional analysis paradigm has roots in feminist analyses (standpoint theory), black feminist thought, postcolonialism, and poststructuralism.

References

Apple, Michael W. 2008. "Curriculum Planning: Content, Form, and the Politics of Accountability." In *The SAGE Handbook of Curriculum and Instruction*, edited by F. Michael Connelly, Ming Fang He, and JoAnn Phillion. Thousand Oaks, CA: Sage. http://www.sage-ereference.com/hdbk_curriculum/Article_n2.html.

Archer, Margaret S. 2012. *The Reflexive Imperative in Late Modernity.* Cambridge: Cambridge University Press. doi:10.1017/CBO9781139108058.

Barnett, Pamela E. 2011. "Discussions Across Difference: Addressing the Affective Dimensions of Teaching Diverse Students about Diversity." *Teaching in Higher Education* 16 (6): 669–679. doi:10.1080/13562517.2011.570435.

Bourdieu, Pierre. 1984. *Distinction: A Social Critique of the Judgement of Taste.* Cambridge: Harvard University Press.

Cabral, Amilcar. 1979. "The *Role* of Culture in the Liberation Struggle." In *Communication and Class Struggle: 1. Capitalism, Imperialism*, edited by Armand Mattelart, and Seth Siegelaub, 205–212. New York, NY: International General.

Cann, Rebecca L., Mark Stoneking, and Allan C. Wilson. 1987. "Mitochondrial DNA and Human Evolution." *Nature*, 325: 31–36. doi:10.1038/325031a0.

Cavalli-Sforza, L. L., P. Menozzi, and A. Piazza. 1994. *The History and Geography of Human Genes.* Princeton, NJ: Princeton University Press.

Clegg, Sue. 2005. "Theorising the Mundane: The Significance of Agency." *International Studies in Sociology of Education* 15(2): 149–164. doi:10.1080/09620210500200137.

Clegg, Sue. 2010. "Time Future – The Dominant Discourse of Higher Education." *Time Society* 19(3): 345–364. doi:10.1177/0961463X10381528.

Clegg, Sue. 2011. "Cultural Capital and Agency: Connecting Critique and Curriculum in Higher Education." *British Journal of Sociology of Education* 32 (1): 93–108. doi:10.1080/01425692.2011.527723.

Coulson, Debra, and Marina Harvey. 2013. "Scaffolding Student Reflection for Experience-Based Learning: A Framework." *Teaching in Higher Education* 18 (4): 401–413. doi:10.1080/13562517.2012.752726.

Cross, Michael. 2004. "Institutionalising Campus Diversity in South African Higher Education: Review of Diversity Scholarship and Diversity Education." *Higher Education* 47 (4): 387–410. doi:10.1023/B:HIGH.0000020854.04852.80.

Denis, Ann. 2008. "Review Essay: Intersectional Analysis: A Contribution of Feminism to Sociology." *International Sociology* 23 (5): 677–694. doi:10.1177/0268580908094468.

Department of Education. 2008. *Report of the Ministerial Committee on Transformation and Social Cohesion and the Elimination of Discrimination in Public Higher Education Institutions.* Pretoria: Department of Education. http://www.pmg.org.za/files/docs/090514racismreport.pdf.

Fanon, Frantz. 1963 *The Wretched of the Earth.* New York, NY: Grove Weidenfeld.

Freire, Paulo. 1973. *Pedagogy of the Oppressed.* New York, NY: The Seabury Press.
Freire, Paulo. 2004. *Pedagogy of Hope: Reliving pedagogy of the oppressed.* New York, NY: Continuum International Publishing.
Greene, Maxine. 2000. *Releasing the Imagination: Essays on Education, the Arts, and Social Change.* San Francisco, CA: Jossey-Bass.
Grumet, Madeleine R. 1980. "Autobiography and Reconceptualization." *The Journal of Curriculum Theorizing* 2 (2): 155–158.
Guha, Ramachandra. 2009. "Words on Water Literature Festival." Introductory paper presented at the morning session 14.9.2009, Durban University of Technology, September 14–15.
Hämäläinen, Raimo, and Esa Saarinen, eds. 2004. *Systems Intelligence: Discovering a Hidden Competence in Human Action and Organizational Life.* Helsinki: Helsinki University of Technology.
Huber, Mary Taylor, and Pat Hutchings. 2005. *Integrative Learning: Mapping the Terrain.* Washington, DC: Association of American Colleges and Universities and the Carnegie Foundation for the Advancement of Teaching: 1–32. www.aacu.org.
Jackson, Norman. 2009. "A Design for Integrative Learning." Surrey Centre for Excellence in Professional Training and Education (SCEPTrE), University of Surrey, Guildford, England. http://www.sceptreserver.co.uk/sceptre/ http://lifewidelearning.pbworks.com/.
Kincheloe, Joe L. 2003. "Critical Ontology: Visions of Selfhood and Curriculum." *Journal of Curriculum Theorizing* 19 (1): 47–64.
Mama, Amina. 1995. *Beyond the Masks: Race, Gender, and Subjectivity.* London: Routledge.
Mama, Amina. 2006. "Towards Academic Freedom for Africa in the 21st Century." *Journal of Higher Education in Africa* 4 (3): 1–32. http://www.codesria.org/IMG/pdf/1-mama-4-3-2006.pdf.
Mamdani, Mahmood. 2007. *Scholars in the Marketplace: The Dilemmas of Neo-Liberal Reform at Makerere University 1989–2005.* Dakar: Codesria.
Mezirow, Jack. 1997. "Transformative Learning: Theory to Practice." *New Directions for Adult and Continuing Education* 74: 5–12. doi:10.1002/ace.7401.
Narismulu, Priya. 1998."'Here Be Dragons': Challenging 'Liberal' Constructions of Protest Poetry." *Alternation* 5 (1): 191–214.
Narismulu, Priya. 1999. "'Unlearning Privilege': Challenging Constructions of Gender and AIDS in Class." *Agenda* 41: 71–78. doi:10.2307/4066201.
Narismulu, Priya. 2000. "What About the Audience? Silences in Voicing the Text." *Alternation* 7 (1): 210–232. http://alternation.ukzn.ac.za/docs/07.1/12%20Nar.pdf.
Narismulu, Priya. 2003. "Examining the Undisclosed Margins: Postcolonial Intellectuals and Subaltern Voices." *Cultural Studies* 17 (1): 56–84. doi:10.1080/0950238032000050832.
Narismulu, Priya. 2009a. "Integrating the Teaching/Research, Theme/Genre Axes: A Postcolonial-Ecofeminist Heuristic." English Studies Research Seminar Series, Durban, Oct 19.
Narismulu, Priya. 2009b. "Springing the Cage: The Postcolonial Ecofeminist Project Engaging the Shades of Robben Island." *Alternation* 16 (2): 265–292. http://alternation.ukzn.ac.za/docs/16.2/17%20Narismulu%20F.PDF.
Narismulu, Priya. 2011. "Teaching Social Justice and Diversity through South/African Stories that Challenge the Chauvinistic Fictions of Apartheid, Patriarchy, Class, Nationalism, Ethnocentrism...." *Alternation* 18 (2): 135–158. http://alternation.ukzn.ac.za/docs/18.2/08%20Nar.pdf.
Nkomo, Mokubung, Derrick Swartz, and Botshabelo Maja, eds. 2006. *Within the Realm of Possibility.* Cape Town: HSRC Press.
Nyamnjoh, Francis B. 2012. "'Potted Plants in Greenhouses': A Critical Reflection on the Resilience of Colonial Education in Africa." *Journal of Asian and African Studies* 47 (2): 129–154. doi:10.1177/0021909611417240.
Ross, Diane. 2007. *Social Justice and Equity: A Teacher Educator's Journey Within.* Paper presented at Inter-American Summit on Conflict Resolution Education (CRE), Cleveland, USA; 25 pp. http://www.tri-c.cc.oh.us/community/gircsummit.htm.

Soudien, Crain. 2010. "Who Takes Responsibility for the 'Reitz Four'? Puzzling Our Way Through Higher Education Transformation in South Africa." *South African Journal of Science* 106 (9/10): 429–436. http://www.sajs.co.za/index.php/SAJS/article/view/429/436.

Spivak, Gayatri. 1990. *The Post-Colonial Critic*. New York, NY: Routledge.

Teferra, Damtew, and Philip G. Altbach. 2004. "African Higher Education: Challenges for the 21st Century." *Higher Education* 47(1): 21–50. doi:10.1023/B:HIGH.0000009822.49980.30.

Vrugt, Anneke, and Frans J. Oort. 2008. "Metacognition, Achievement Goals, Study Strategies and Academic Achievement: Pathways to Achievement." *Metacognition Learning* 3 (2): 123–146. doi:10.1007/s11409-008-9022-4.

The influence of internationalisation and national identity on teaching and assessments in higher education

Jane Vinther and Gordon Slethaug

Language and Communication, University of Southern Denmark, Odense, Denmark; English Language and Literature, University of Waterloo, Waterloo, Canada

Recent and current changes in higher education have been both top-down and bottom-up, i.e. regulation and control measures from authorities on one hand and increasing numbers of international students on the other. This has led to a dilemma between unification and diversification. There is a marked pressure towards more testing, more streamlining and less autonomy. This development is caused by both top-down regulation and increasing diversity in the student body. This paper will examine the consequent impact on pedagogy and assessment, current practices and educational philosophies. We aim to ask questions pertinent to the substantial values and goals of our higher education institutions and to begin a discussion of the what, why and how of the renewal process. In particular, it discusses the effects in relation to teacher and learner autonomy in an intercultural classroom with multiple languages, expectation and traditions.

Internationalisation and globalisation are on everyone's minds these days and, in certain respects, have inspired educational renewal in universities. Moreover, the increasing numbers of international students who move from their familiar cultural environment to participate in educational programmes abroad, currently over six million annually (Slethaug 2010, 1), bring with them expectations and experiences that can benefit the receiving educational institutions despite increased complexity in administration. Nonetheless, there are important questions that institutions, regulators and individual lecturers need to bring to the forefront. Values, beliefs and practices need to be clarified institutionally and even nationally to create a mutually fruitful and genuine conversation. It would be beneficial and uplifting if the situation could be turned into an opening for reflection for the parties involved.

To begin this conversation, this essay will examine: different theories of, and attitudes to, internationalisation, including unification and diversification, convergence and divergence, and the symbolic and transformative; the framework of national heritage, in this case Danish, and the pillars on which it rests; an assessment of how traditions and pedagogical practices, exemplified by testing, are being affected by internationalisation; and the possibilities for renewal along with an appraisal of core values of student and teacher autonomy. This essay intends to cast a critical eye on the forces which motor the processes with seemingly little involvement from educational research and the pedagogical community, and it is from this point of departure that we advocate inclusion of voices rooted in the classroom.

Internationalisation: unification or diversification, convergence or divergence, symbolic or transformative

The coming together of people, ideas and cultures may lead to genuinely transformative internationalisation 'integrating "an international/intercultural dimension into the teaching, research and service functions of academic institutions"' (Schweisfurth and Gu 2009, 463), or it may lead to a merely 'symbolic' transformation, involving a scramble for international funds or even systemic clashes involving style, content and pedagogical frameworks within higher education (HE). Though Nybom (2007) sees the massification in the late twentieth century as one factor that has impacted significantly on higher education, he is not optimistic about a European transformation. In his opinion, research universities in the US have been proactive in responding to increasing numbers of students, but European universities have been reactive (Nybom 2007, 72), letting massification, internationalisation and European harmonisation set the stage for educational change. This has led to an unthinking unification, convergence and symbolic change, as opposed to an incorporation of diversification, divergence and transformation.

On the unification side, the flow of international students has become big business across the globe, and universities do not want to miss out on that action, as indicated by statistics from four important receiving countries. In 2008, 671,000 international universities students studied in the US, generating revenue of $16 billion. In 2011, 400,000 international university students studied in the UK, generating £14 billion in revenue. In 2009, 207,000 international students studied in Australia, generating $16.5 billion in revenue. And in 2011, 178,000 international students studied in Canada, generating $6.8 billion in revenue.

These numbers mean that universities are 'steered by the criteria of socio-economic usefulness' and 'the adoption of a corporatist governance and management model, which has created a new top-down line management structure' (Kim 2009, 397), affecting not only students but the professoriate. For instance, as a result of administrative policy at Oxford University, one third of the students and half of the newly hired faculty are now international, resulting in diversification of cultural backgrounds, knowledge and work methods as well as a 'de-nationalization of the profession' (Kim 2009, 398), which has a price – the loss of autonomy, independence and possibly 'transformative' change (Schweisfurth and Gu 2009, 463). In Europe, this HE unification and denationalisation have been driven by central EU decisions outside the traditions of the nation states and universities, but subsequently enforced and implemented by the universities.

Altogether, such changes mean that universities across the globe are moving in concert, driven by similar internal structures and external dynamics, a perfect example of convergence:

> The convergence hypothesis builds on the assumption that although there are differences between nations and between organizations, such differences are relatively insignificant

> compared to the forces that press societies and organizations to align themselves toward the same economic and technological structures. (Cheney et al. 2011, 404)

The forces of unification and convergence are propelled by macro-political and organizational forces in contrast to divergence and diversification which primarily flow from individuals and groups who work within local cultural boundaries. The auto-velocity of either path impacts on study programmes, courses and lecturers, but without much discussion or planning by the professoriate. Paradoxically, then, the more varied the student body becomes, the stronger is the call for more international standardisation, unification and convergence in goals, teaching methodology, evaluation, testing and assessment. This raises important questions in relation to HE trajectories and their impact on local, national and global identities.

Ideology and pedagogy

The literature on education often creates contrasting typologies of Western and Eastern/Asian educational traditions, practices and value systems, implying that 'Western' describes a uniform approach to teaching and learning embracing critical thinking and independent work to create well-educated and democratic members of society. Many scholars query the assumption that 'Western' can describe a single rubric, but the EU is currently welding many different nation-states into a more or less single force for education.

Little heed is paid to scholars who go against this ideology, though Leathwood and others (Leathwood 2006; Leathwood and O'Connell 2003; Johnson, Lee, and Green 2000; Fraser and Gordon 1997) have questioned such concepts, including those of student autonomy and independence, pointing out vast differences in values based on gender, class and race. Our position in this essay is to highlight the limited inclusion of diverse values, philosophies and practices.

The Bologna process was adopted by the EU to initiate unification, streamline HE ground rules, and thereby facilitate student exchanges and the transfer of credits across national systems while enhancing intercultural knowledge and understanding. The various EU exchange programmes have been successful in many of these respects, but experiences of students and lecturers make it clear that differences still abound in philosophy, didactic principles, and practices as well as in testing and assessment, and Nybom warns against believing that the Bologna process 'will, in itself, . . . raise the quality of higher education' (2007, 77).

Regarding typologies, it seems clear that southern Europe and northern Europe adhere to different beliefs and philosophies. In written and oral surveys at a Danish university, students from Spain and France note, for example, that class discussion and group work among students are common in Denmark but not usual in their home countries where the authority and dominance of the teacher are higher.

In Denmark, there are tacit values informing the HE classroom that stem from the middle of the nineteenth century built on Nikolaj Grundtvig's notion that both teachers and students should have independence and autonomy in their pursuit of knowledge and educational goals. As Vinther and Slethaug have noted (2012), this view grew out of Wilhelm Von Humboldt's late eighteenth-century view of *Bildung* – that education was not to be based upon Latin-school notions of memorisation but rather more independent thinking to develop an educated person who could contribute freely to the new knowledge, democratic ideals and civic society that was forming in the wake of the Enlightenment. As Klafki remarks, the concept of *Bildung* was based upon empiricism and reason, independence of science and research and, consequently, free and independent universities:

> Bildung is understood as a qualification for reasonable self-determination, which presupposes and includes emancipation from determination by others. It is a qualification for autonomy, for freedom for individual thought, and for individual moral decisions. Precisely because of this, creative self-activity is the central form in which the process of Bildung is carried out. (2000, 87)

A person educated in this manner was to become well informed and cultured, independent in life and able to construct and live by important educational, social and spiritual values. To accomplish this, institutions of higher learning needed to integrate these values at all levels.

Didaktik (the German spelling current in Germany and Scandinavia today) signifies this belief as developed in northern Europe and Scandinavia. As Vinther and Slethaug remark:

> autonomy and independence of teachers are key conditions for the focus on the content, including the selection and mediation of the content for the benefit of the students. In the Humboldtian-*didaktik* tradition the content is in focus insofar as the didactic deliberations serve the purpose of aiding the teacher in enhancing the learning of the students. (2012, 61)

This educational tradition has held together for a remarkably long period, though it is now held in place by a general social understanding rather than read through these German or Danish philosophers.

Other modes of education in continental northern Europe influenced by the Humboldtian university ideals of democratisation and autonomy have found diverse forms in different countries. It is this diversity that forces of unification and convergence are trying to minimise for utilitarian purposes. A recent publication (Ozga et al. 2011) brings to light some of the significant differences in northern Europe, indeed, even within the Scandinavian countries. In examining attitudes among teachers at pre-university level in five northern countries – England, Finland, Scotland, Sweden and Denmark – this team found significant differences in teachers' perception of the most important qualities in education. Typically, Danish teachers found it important that students became democratically formed and that they were involved in their own learning, while teachers in Scotland and Finland emphasised the importance of skills acquisition. In contrast to the teachers in England, Scotland, Sweden and Finland, Danish teachers found international testing comparisons, such as PISA, to have a negative impact on teaching quality, suggesting systemic differences in educational philosophy.

In their respective publications, Hamilton and Gundem have individually outlined the fundamental differences between educational beliefs, including those in the triangle of Anglo-American, northern European and southern European traditions, even down to a difference in the definition and presence of the concept of pedagogy. This paper adheres to the definition of Hamilton and Zufiaurre (2000, 5; see also Bernstein 1971; Simon 1981):

> 'Pedagogy' refers to the integration in practice of particular curriculum content and design, classroom strategies and techniques, and evaluation, purposes and methods. All of these aspects of educational practice come together in the realities of what happens in classroom. Together, they organize a view of how a teacher's work within an institutional context specifies a particular version of what knowledge is of most worth, what it means to know something, and how we might construct representation of ourselves, others and our physical and social environment.

In its interpretation of this tradition, Danish HE implies that teaching should be research-based and that the construction of self and society should arise from a fusion of democratic and formative purposes of education. The ideals of democratic participation and conversation between agents permeate the pedagogical beliefs, curriculum planning, syllabus creation and teaching practices throughout the Danish systemic and institutional frameworks. Pivotal in the process, the lecturer holds disciplinary information and interprets the educational framework in which course content is to be mediated (Vinther 2010).

Given this philosophy, the lecturer served institutional decision-makers in ensuring appropriate methods of instruction, testing and assessment. The choice of content and testing – and the correlation between them – thus were not decided by politicians, administrators and statisticians at the expense of the lecturer. Nonetheless, in local and national contexts, this was a field fraught with potential problems and conflicts. If added dimensions of European harmony and internationalisation are introduced, the complexity multiplies, making consultations between the various levels in the process indispensable but sometimes overlooked or ignored. The political pressures for alignment and harmonisation beg for reflections on the qualities and core values we want from our current educational tradition, though these fail to happen.

In particular, for the humanities, it appears pertinent to discuss the inherent values we perceive in liberal education and its double purpose of education and social formation in contrast to a more utilitarian approach to education; furthermore, we might consider how testing and assessment should reflect those values, and how we could operationalise this in a sound pedagogical framework informed by internationalisation.

Independence and autonomy or utilitarianism

Although the Humboldtian ideal has not yet come under fire in Denmark, it has in other places. A decade ago, Leathwood and O'Connell challenged the value of autonomy in the UK HE, linking the desire for independence to 'masculinist conceptions of the individual, with this learner constructed as male, white, middle class and able bodied' (2003, 599). Leathwood herself followed up implications of this claim in noting that the discourse of development from dependence to independence and the insistence on individualism, self-reliance, self-confidence and rationality are drawn from and lend support to the New Right in the UK and follow similar premises of American neo-liberal thinking. She thus finds that these discourses not only comprise an idealised 'critical consciousness' of the classroom but also the politicised mantra of the right-wing elite in the UK who use it to cut educational budgets. These objections are well worth considering and constitute reminders that there are many subtle and contradictory valences in the terms 'Western', 'independence' and 'autonomy'.

With such challenges, then, this northern European tradition may be eroding, so the question is whether policies of internationalisation, diversity in the student body, unification and structural changes make it a feasible goal or whether there are other approaches that ought to be considered. In the opinion of Woolf (2009, 58), who quotes Dickens' character Gradgrind from *Hard Times*, we have entered a new 'utilitarian' era that has replaced the earlier focus on independence. Figures and facts, which are easily measured and entered into taxonomies and tables, dominate the debate. Policy-makers and economic considerations create the conditions in which educational institutions are trying to manoeuvre. International students need to pass exams and to bring home credits while simultaneously having satisfactory cultural and personal experiences. This puts external pressure on the universities, and the structural changes necessitated by internationalisation will have causal effects on internal pressures to adopt curriculum, testing and course assessment. Woolf concludes that 'success in international education may be measured as long as we recognise that the outcomes are partial and usually driven by an agenda beyond the purely educational' (2009, 63). In the same vein, Hudzik and Stohl (2009, 11) maintain that:

> Entities throughout the world that fund higher education are under increasing pressure to deliver value-for-money, both by constraining recourses to extract greater efficiency and by requiring certain outcomes (e.g., graduation rates, student performance on standardised tests, faculty research and instructional productivity).

There is a pronounced pressure to increase the number of international students, accelerate students who lag behind and reduce drop-out rates. These are goals in their own right, but they have become measuring points in the contractual agreements between universities and the government. The number of international students, study time and dropout rates are three aspects that, compared to those in natural sciences and social sciences, have recently put the humanities in an unfavourable light, giving prominence to forces which strive towards unification, streamlining, testing and applications in parallel with the sciences.

Dynamic change is inevitable for the university in general and humanities in particular but might, in the northern European context at least, be expected to take up a debate about the legacy from a tradition less focused on quantifiable and easily tested skills. The resulting conversation about civic values, an indispensable core of the humanities, on the one hand, and a curriculum constructed and assessed in a utilitarian fashion, on the other hand, could result in a modern and international curriculum with appropriately related teaching and assessment methods. Curriculum development to be viable for the future needs to be situated in, and based upon, a new interpretation of inclusiveness and dialogue.

Internationalisation, teaching and testing

Until the advent of educational internationalisation, national educational philosophies arguably found expression in a combination of content, teaching methods, testing and assessment. In theory at least, there was a national purpose and coherence among them, with teachers granted the trust of the educational system to provide valid methods of assessment to ensure quality and fairness. Breaking this connection would breach the social contract between policy-makers, teachers, students and society at large.

This national imperative is being challenged by an increasingly international agenda based mainly upon a demonstration of skills, with standardised testing rather than holistic assessment, and Grundy for one (1987, 77) has warned against the consequences of making skill demonstration the object of pedagogy in the context of a process-learning approach to science. In the humanities, this is even more critical. However, skill demonstration appears to be on the rise, supported by policymakers looking towards internationalisation as the great unifier. The tendency away from nationally or regionally based pedagogy towards policy-based frameworks might well alter the coherence between teaching, pedagogy and the ideals of autonomy and social involvement. The teacher as resource of knowledge of content, students and appropriate assessment methods based in national consensus might become a thing of the past, diminishing autonomy of both students and teachers. The socio-cultural conversation might become deprived of its meaningfulness, not allowing 'students and teachers together to confront the real problems of their existence and relationships' (Grundy 1987, 105). In a broader perspective, it might ruin the ability of the students to enter into an evaluation of their own situation with regard to learning as well as life, making them less equipped to participate in the comprehensive dialogue and discussion of society and less confident in their contribution to democratic sustainment and the development of the values on which to build future educational achievements.

In language learning and teaching, this kind of 'Western' skill-oriented unification process has been pronounced, as exemplified by the Common European Framework of Reference (CEFR).[1] An increasing number of research articles and policy papers highlight the CEFR's basic 'can-do' tables for six levels of users, from beginners to those who are proficient; this process, according to the Committee of Ministers, aims 'to achieve greater unity among its members . . . by the adoption of common action in the cultural field' (CEFR document, 2), but this current tendency is unproductive in that the CEFR is erringly thought to be a valid set of descriptors that can be exploited by relating classroom teaching to testing of proficiencies as described in the 'can-do' tables. This is a less than productive approach for three reasons. First, the general-level descriptions are far too imprecise to be used as testing matrices. Second, the imprecision leaves a given set of concepts open to interpretation. And third, the CEFR by its very nature is de-contextualised and not observant of national traditions and educational practices. The Council for Cultural Co-operation of the Council of Europe (2001) hails the 'rich heritage of diverse languages and cultures,' and yet it advocates 'greater convergence at the European level by means of appropriate arrangements for ongoing co-operation and co-ordination of policies' (CEFR document, 2). The CEFR document illustrates the dilemma which is the theme of this paper, namely, the paradox that diversity leads to unification and convergence.

A glance at the C1 and C2 levels of writing (Figure 1) makes it abundantly clear that this is far too general and imprecise to be the basis of testing, especially high-stakes testing, and that the concepts are less than salient. In addition, research shows that different educational systems have different interpretations of levels and competencies. The CEFR is, in essence, a taxonomy of communicative skills rather

C1

I can express myself in clear, well-structured text, […]I can select style appropriate to the reader in mind.

I can write about complex subjects in a letter, an essay or a report, underlining what I consider to be the salient issues

C2

I can write clear, smoothly flowing text in an appropriate style.

I can write complex letters, reports or articles which present a case with an effective logical structure which helps the recipient to notice and remember significant points

Figure 1. Excerpt from CEFR grid. (Colours applied by authors to ease comparison of the two level statements).

than an expression of academic ability, and its application as a testing taxonomy problematic.

Together, these issues stemming from the CEFR are illustrative in two ways: they demonstrate the importance of situated assessment and the need to adapt assessment to the type of knowledge to be assessed; plus, they make it clear that higher education has a responsibility beyond skill development and that this responsibility in the light of both national identity and internationalisation needs to be focused on a process of pedagogical evaluation completely absent from 'can-do' taxonomies. The inherent problem with top-down convergence measures such as the CEFR is that in order to encompass any deviating eventuality, they, by nature, need to be so general that they become meaningless. The pressures of internationalisation make it paramount that each national educational hierarchy responds with an examination and deliberation of its own values and priorities in order to decide where to incorporate and adapt to external forces and where to insist on renewal from a firm stand on one's heritage.

In a report on internationalisation in education (2011), the Accreditation Organisation of the Netherlands and Flanders (NVAO) points out that internationalisation should be based on a *vision* of internationalisation, that this vision should reflect diversity, that individual programmes may have different visions and objectives, and that the operationalisation of internationalisation must spring from local programme features:

> The programme's desired internationalisation must have a significant impact on the overall quality of the programme. Internationalisation, at least in the context of a distinctive quality feature, should not just be an end in itself but the programme should clarify how internationalisation contributes to the overall quality of the programme. (Aerden, Frederiks, and van den Heuvel 2011, 6).

Incorporating European and/or international test frameworks or methods is not in itself a satisfactory way forward; pedagogical deliberations, course content, methods and outcomes need a more thorough and coherent process of development (Weir 2005).

Humanities have the inherent obligation to insist on reflecting on all its work, objects of scrutiny, and operations, including self-reflection – not because humanities areas are privileged or above the rules governing higher education, but because of its *raison d'être*. Consequently, visions for curriculum development with consequences for content, pedagogy and assessment need to include a discussion of the global community, 'Western' society and values (including independence, autonomy, and democracy), national and personal identity, and educational philosophy, among others. An aim to engage students in their own learning and foster problem-solving and respect for a variety of viewpoints follow naturally from such conversations in democratic education in which teacher and student work together towards a common goal of knowledge (Slater 2004).

Around the globe universities are trying to tap into globalisation: 'They all want to become "excellent" and "world class"; they all want to be research-led' (Biesta 2011, 37), but internationalisation is not the preserve of any one university or government. Collectively, universities have achieved much-needed change and adaptation to new world realities, but now the way forward is to put that together with a university's/nation's uniqueness and inherited tradition: being aware that higher education has a wider, international perspective must go hand in hand with an affirmation of underlying local values and beliefs.

Reducing higher education to a question of acquisition of facts or skills, as discussed above, would alter the humanities and constitute a setback for liberal education in the Humboldtian sense. In that tradition, there has been freedom for lecturers to choose their methodology, interpret their knowledge and research and elect their pedagogy. Their informed views on the assessment appropriate for given courses and knowledge have previously been given room and voice. In the humanities in Denmark, the acknowledged form of assessment has often been an essay in which the students would combine the knowledge and insights gained throughout the study period with critical thinking and critiques of existing research in the field, regarded as a natural continuation of the dialogical interaction between the teacher, the student and the material. This educational philosophy allows autonomy for the lecturer and independence for the student in their production of knowledge. Students with international backgrounds often comment positively on this process in evaluations and surveys, finding this autonomy of independent work both elevating and challenging, though they come from systems with different academic traditions. One international student apologised for her lack of participation this way: 'I just want to inform that I am sorry for just listening [to] your lecture, always', indicating that she would like to have entered into the discussion but wasn't comfortable enough with this change from practices in her home culture. Within the Danish system, the privilege of autonomy holds an inherent obligation to engage in an ongoing conversation to bring forward the formative content towards the educational ideals of *Bildung*.

Tange (2010) suggests that the international classroom be used as a resource in which such diversity is incorporated by the lecturers in their management of learning. This falls into the tradition of Grundtvig's idea of what education should be and seems to suggest that, if we apply the right strategies, our educational development will build on added value, carrying forward integrity and relevance.

Danes, like everyone else, are formed by their educational system and underlying values, tacitly or explicitly. To some degree, this has given Danes the perception that exact, item-based knowledge and competition about knowledge are not as valuable as the ability to discuss, cooperate, work in groups and focus on lifting everyone rather than getting ahead oneself. The belief is that applied and ready knowledge can be acquired after learning how and where to acquire it and being given the means to assess it critically. This perception has been inherent in teaching, learning, testing, and assessment as well as in the attitude of parents, teachers, and instructional frameworks. The right, indeed the obligation, of teachers as well as students, to develop the potential of every single person and personality must be the first priority. Currently, this is being questioned in several ways, institutionally and pedagogically.

The unification and convergence tendencies derived from international testing set-ups such as PISA and the EU governmental-level testing for civil-servant entrance requirements show that Danes are left behind in contexts in which they see themselves as natural members and agents. The pressure also comes from the influx of international students from educational systems which adhere to an educational philosophy founded in unified testing systems and credits. This is happening at the same time as internationalisation of education, whether we like it or not, has become a global commodity, and the students who follow this global flow expect value for money in the form of diplomas, credits and exam papers.

Furthermore, the academic requirements of the internationalised student body cannot be met if their diversity does not take into account their needs. In a sense, it makes the lecturers hostage in a no-man's land between ideals and reality. The institutions of higher education need to realise the predicament of individual lecturers in the face of the academic tradition of involvement, problem-solving, discussion and inclusion, and the demands they face from individual students. Pedagogical development needs to be facilitated to fit the new realities of internationalised higher education by encouraging participation and by establishing support for an institutional framework of change in related exam forms and adapted assessment methods.

There is a need to re-evaluate the content of programmes and to create coherence between different types of knowledge and assessments. Despite our instincts, not all knowledge needs to be problematised and discussed; not all exams need to be elaborate; and not all essays original. We need to create progression in complexity, not only in types of content, types of knowledge, but also in types of assessment.

It is time to discuss in a balanced way which values we believe to be worth preserving in our educational philosophy. Our legacy needs to be appraised from the new global perspective in order to establish how we can preserve what we deem to be unique qualities, not just for our own sake but also because we can contribute something of value to others. In higher education, established approaches need to be re-appraised at intervals in relation to current conditions. In some respects, this may result in diminished surface autonomy for lecturers and students; however, it may also bring more autonomy in the sense that the energy and initiative of both students and lecturers can be employed in more innovative and meaningful pursuits. We need to differentiate and diversify in order to modernize and adapt in areas where it makes sense and does not lead to a sell-out of core values. Diversity and divergence vs. unification and convergence cannot be resolved by applying learning methods from one system to another if these do not fit the competencies and knowledge types that one wants to test. Similarly, particular teaching and learning methods may not bring forth the best capabilities of the test-takers if they are not comfortable with them, or if any cultural or linguistic issues block the possibility of the student from drawing on important knowledge that needs to be displayed and assessed.

Conclusion

Probably, no one wants to turn the clock back twenty years when most of the students in any given country belonged to a single nationality. We have all benefited immensely from the flow of students, researchers and faculty members across the globe. To that extent, unification and convergence have transformed universities in positive ways. However, we also must be sure that we do not allow EU socio-economic values and pragmatism to swamp our national pedagogical and institutional values. It is time to have a debate about what those values are and how we can blend internationalisation with them to make stronger, more interesting higher education that can either demonstrate internationalisation with local characteristics or local higher education with international characteristics. Then, we may well have the best of unification and diversity and convergence and divergence.

Note

1. http://www.coe.int/t/DG4/Portfolio/documents/Framework_EN.pdf.

References

Aerden, A., M. Frederiks, and E. van den Heuvel. 2011. "The Methodology Applied." In *The Assessment of Internationalisation*, edited by L. Bollaert, 4–16. The Hague: Accreditation Organisation of the Netherlands and Flanders (NVAO – Nederlands-Vlaamse Accreditatie-organisatie). http://nvao.com/news/item/frameworks_for_the_assessment_of_internationalisation_and_evaluation_report_published/44.

Bernstein, B. 1971. "On The Classification and Training of Educational Knowledge." In *Knowledge and Control: New Directions for the Sociology of Knowledge*, edited by M. F. D. Young, 44–69. London: Collier-Macmillan.

Biesta, G. 2011. "How Useful Should the University Be? On the Rise of the Global University and the Crisis in Higher Education." *Qui Parle* 20 (1): 35–47. doi:10.5250/quiparle.20.1.0035.

Cheney, G., L.T. Christensen, T. E. Zorn Jr., and S. Ganesh. 2011. *Organizational Communication in an Age of Globalization: Issues, Reflections, Practices*. Long Grove, IL: Waveland Press.

Council of Europe, Strasbourg. 2001. *Common European Framework of References for Languages: Learning, Teaching, Assessment*. Cambridge University Press. http://www.coe.int/t/DG4/Portfolio/documents/Framework_EN.pdf.

Fraser, N., and L. Gordon. 1997. "A Genealogy of 'Dependency': Tracing a Keyword of the US Welfare State." In *Justice Interruptus: Critical Reflections on the 'Postsocialist' Condition*, edited by N. Fraser, 121–149. New York: Routledge.

Grundy, S. 1987. *Curriculum: Product or Praxis*. Lewes: Falmer.

Hamilton, D., and B. Zufiaurre. 2000. "The New Pedagogics: Revisiting Curriculum and Didactics." Paper presented at the Annual Meeting of the American Educational Research Association, New Orleans, April 24–28.

Hudzik, J. K., and M. Stohl. 2009. "Modelling Assessment of the Outcomes and Impacts of Internationalisation." In *Measuring Success in the Internationalisation of Higher Education: EAIE Occasional Paper 22*, edited by H. de Wit, 9–21. Amsterdam: European Association for International Education.

Johnson, L., A. Lee, and B. Green. 2000. "The PhD and the Autonomous Self: Gender, Rationality and Postgraduate Pedagogy." *Studies in Higher Education* 25 (2): 135–147. doi:10.1080/713696141.

Kerr, C. 1991. *The Great Transformation in Higher Education: 1960–1980*. Albany: State University of New York Press.

Kim, T. 2009. "Transnational Academic Mobility, Internationalization and Interculturality in Higher Education." *Intercultural Education* 20 (5): 395–405. doi:10.1080/14675980903371241.

Klafki, W. 2000. "The Significance of Classical Theories of Bildung for a Contemporary Concept of Allgemeinbildung." In *Teaching as a Reflective Practice*, edited by I. Westbuty, S. Hopmann, and K. Riquarts, 85–107. Mahwah, NJ: Lawrence Erlbaum.

Leathwood, C. 2006. "Gender, Equity and the Discourse of the Independent Learner in Higher Education." *Higher Education* 52 (4): 611–633. doi:10.1007/s10734-005-2414-3.

Leathwood, C., and P. O'Connell. 2003. "'It's a Struggle': The Construction of the 'New Student' in Higher Education." *Journal of Education Policy* 18 (6): 597–615. doi:10.1080/0268093032000145863.

Nybom, T. 2007. "A Rule-governed Community of Scholars: The Humboldt Vision in the History of the European University." In *University dynamics and European Integration*, edited by P. Maasen and J. P. Olsen, 55–80. Berlin: Springer.

Ozga, J., P. Dahler-Larsen, C. Segerhold, and S. Hannu, eds. 2011. *Fabricating Quality in Education. Data and Governance in Europe*. London and New York: Routledge.

Schweisfurth, M., and Q. Gu. 2009. "Exploring the Experiences of International Students in UK Higher Education: Possibilities and Limits of Interculturality in University Life." *Intercultural Education* 20 (5): 463–473. doi:10.1080/14675980903371332.

Simon, B. 1981. "Why no Pedagogy in England?." In *Education in the Eighties*, edited by B. Simon and W. Taylor, 124–145. London: Batsford.

Slater, L. 2004. "Relationship-driven Teaching Cultivates Collaboration and Inclusion." *Kappa Delta Pi Record* 40 (2): 58–59. doi:10.1080/00228958.2004.10517287.

Slethaug, G. 2010. "Introduction." In *International Education and the Chinese Learner*, edited by J. Ryan and G. Slethaug, 1–12. Hong Kong: Hong Kong University Press.

Tange, H. 2010. "Caught in the Tower of Babel: University Lecturers' Experiences with Internationalisation." *Language and Intercultural Communication* 10 (2): 137–149. doi:10.1080/14708470903342138.

Vinther, J. 2010. "A Danish Perspective on Teaching Chinese Students in Europe." In *International Education and the Chinese Learner*, edited by J. Ryan and G. Slethaug, 11–127. Hong Kong: Hong Kong University Press.

Vinther, J., and G. Slethaug. 2012. "The Danish Educational Tradition: Multiple Heritages and International Challenges and Conversation." In *Researching Intercultural Learning: Investigations in Language and Education*, edited by M. Cortazzi and L. Jin, 58–77. London and New York: Palgrave Macmillan.

Weir, C. J. 2005. "Limitations of the Common European Framework for Developing Comparable Examinations and Tests." *Language Testing* 22 (3): 281–300. doi:10.1191/0265532205lt309oa.

Woolf, M. 2009. "Measuring Success in Education Abroad: Who are We Trying to Impress?" In *Measuring Success in the Internationalisation of Higher Education*, edited by H. de Wit, 57–64. Amsterdam: European Association for International Education.

Online teaching communities within sociology: a counter trend to the marketization of higher education

Nathan Palmer and April M. Schueths

Department of Sociology and Anthropology, Georgia Southern University, Statesboro, USA

As higher education embraces the ideologies of the market, educators are being asked to teach evermore students with fewer resources. Running counter to the trend of marketization, a decentralized group of educators are taking advantage of Web 2.0 technologies (including Facebook, Twitter, and blogging platforms such as Wordpress, etc.) to collaborate online to share teaching resources, support one another, and improve pedagogy. Open Educational Resources (OERs) are online collections of pedagogical content/media that are freely distributed. In addition to resources, communities of educators are coming together to support one another and provide informal mentoring in what we call Online Teaching Community Networks (OTCNs). We review how OERs and OTCNs are forming within the discipline of sociology to illustrate the potential both have to improve pedagogy and support teachers.

Introduction

Rapid changes are taking place within higher education in the wake of the global economic downturn and an international shift toward marketization (Barnett 2010; Nickolai, Hoffman, and Trautner 2012). This draws into question the role higher education plays in society and the value teachers have within it. Teaching faculties in many places have been devalued, compared to their researching counterparts (Anderson et al. 2011). An increasing proportion of student education is being shouldered by contingent faculty who focus primarily on instruction (Eurostat 2010; Schuster 2011). At the same time resources for teaching are shrinking while class sizes and course loads grow (Monks and Schmidt 2010).

The public is demanding that higher education become 'better, faster, and cheaper' (Schejbal 2012, 1). 'We have to do more with less', is the nearly singular message coming from leadership in higher education. From both outside and within higher education there is pressure to adopt the values, practices, and technologies of the market (Deem 1998).

However, while it is undeniable that teachers in higher education face tightening constraints, the changing landscape also affords educators new opportunities. With the development of online technologies such as Facebook, Twitter, and blogging platforms like Wordpress, often referred to collectively by the umbrella terms social media or Web 2.0, educators now have the opportunity to form communities to collaborate with one another in ways unimaginable to previous generations. Educators around the world have seized this opportunity and formed decentralized informal teaching communities fueled by a passion for teaching and a spirit of 'gift giving' (Bouwma-Gearhart and Bess 2012, 270). These communities provide support, informal mentoring, and resources for teaching and represent an opportunity for faculty to reduce the burden they face by collaborating to offset a portion of their workload. While Web 2.0 technologies have been widely embraced outside academia, they have only recently begun to gain the attention of educational researchers and teachers (Hung and Yuen 2010). Scholars have primarily examined the impact of Web 2.0 technologies on primary and secondary teacher training (Sun 2010), student learning (Tan and Pearce 2012), and have been slower to explore its impact on teaching in higher education.

A large portion of research in this area focuses on Open Educational Resources (OERs) which is a broad term coined by the United Nations to denote everything from free and open 'courseware' (i.e. resources for an entire class) (e.g. Connexions) to repositories of activities, assignments, and syllabi (e.g. MERLOT, Jorum Open) (Bossu and Tynan 2011; Weller 2011). As OERs infoKit suggests, 'There is no one, standard definition of [OERs]'.

Within departments and across institutions, faculty has always shared resources and provided support to one another, at least to some degree. Research suggests that teaching communities like these play a vital role in advancing pedagogy and that teaching in isolation is not ideal (Spalter-Roth et al. 2010). Macdonald (2001) found that participation in a formal teaching community for engineers lead to a 'substantial morale boost for some disillusioned staff who were finding the recent changes to university teaching conditions depressing' (161). Similarly, Hunt, Mair, and Atkinson (2012) reported that both formal and informal teaching communities aided sociology graduate students in developing teaching abilities and identities. Furthermore, many disciplines have formed sections within their national network to promote quality teaching.

While the research on OERs often mentions the potential they have for interaction and community formation, this aspect deserves more than an incidental analysis. In addition to distributing resources, Web 2.0 technologies have dramatically increased the ease with which individuals can interact. Academics have seized the opportunities afforded by Web 2.0 technologies to create both formal and informal communities to support pedagogy and each other.

We are arguing that the communities of educators online serve similar functions as offline and face-to-face teacher community networks. Presently, the OER research insufficiently grapples with the social and community aspects of the networks of teachers forming online. To this end we advocate for borrowing from the research on Teaching Community Networks (TCNs) (Hunt, Mair, and Atkinson 2012) and expanding it to include the aspects unique to an online community; we call these groups of educators as Online Teaching Community Networks (OTCNs).

OERs and OTCNs represent a counter trend within the context of the marketization of higher education; a trend in line with Danaher, Gale, and Erben's (2000, 26) call for teachers to, 'lead the way rather than allow themselves to be steered down paths they do not particularly want to go'. Within the discipline of sociology, multiple OERs and OTCNs have emerged that demonstrates how when teachers work collaboratively they can advance pedagogy, support one another, and even engage the general public.

Teaching during precarious times

A cursory glance at The Chronicle of Higher Education or at recent titles such as, 'The lost soul of higher education: corporatization, the assault on academic freedom, and the end of the American University' (Schrecker 2010); 'In search of a new paradigm for higher education' (Schejbal 2012), etc. suggests that higher education is in a precarious position. Scholars both validate the sentiment in these titles as well as challenge them. 'The academy has been undergoing an accelerated rate of change, almost surely at an unprecedented pace' (Sinclair and Levett-Jones 2011, 4) yet others argue that institutions of higher education are perpetually in a state of change and perceived crisis (Thelin 2011).

Some of the current challenges teachers in higher education face center on changing workforce dynamics, such as an increase in the disproportionate growth of administrators and noneducators relative to tenure track faculty (Ginsberg 2011) and the reliance on contingent faculty (Kezar and Sam 2010). Although the use of part-time faculty members has been increasing for some time, it should give us all pause that the majority of new full-time appointees regardless of institution type are nontenure teaching positions (American Association of University Professors 2003; Sinclair and Levett-Jones 2011). This has led some to argue that the tenure process, including the protections of academic freedom, is on the way out.

Faculty workloads that have traditionally focused on teaching, research, and service are also changing. Tenured faculty, especially at research intensive institutions are expected to publish research and secure lucrative grants, and some argue, to the detriment of teaching (Anderson et al. 2011). Teaching is, 'generally not perceived as being significantly rewarded' (Arum and Roska 2011, 12). Contingent faculty are primarily tasked with student education (Sinclair and Levett-Jones 2011) and often work under some of the most difficult conditions. For example, adjunct faculty are often assigned their courses only a few weeks before the term begins with little time to prepare their classes (Street et al. 2012). Not surprisingly as faculty bifurcate either into a teaching or research focus their compensation follows (Sinclair and Levett-Jones 2011, 12). As the global economic recession continues and public funds dry up, the pressure for faculty to pull in external funding intensifies while simultaneously so too does the pressure to cut costs by hiring contingent faculty on less costly contracts (AFT Higher Education 2009; Basken 2011).

Many scholars argue that the driving force behind the changes within higher education stem from the increasing use of the values of economics in the institution in what is known as the 'marketization of higher education'. Nickolai, Hoffman, and Trautner (2012, 214) asks 'whether a value-set that privileges knowledge creation and learning is being overtaken by economic instrumentalism'. Marketization has saturated all realms of higher education and has become a visible worldwide phenomenon, especially in the USA and the UK with Continental Europe and Asian countries also moving in that direction (Barnett 2010, 40; Oplatka and Hemsley-Brown 2010; Xiong 2012). Critics argue that the marketization of higher education has disempowered faculty (Glowacki-Dudka and Brown 2007) and reduced their role within higher education to producing consumers rather than scholars (Molesworth, Nixon, and Scullion 2009).

However, not all scholars write off the marketization of higher education as patently bad. Barnett (2010, 50) suggests that there is opportunity in this predicament, 'It is possible not that just the pernicious aspects of marketization can be ameliorated but also that its virtuous aspects can be heightened. This is perhaps the crucial pedagogical challenge of our times'.

Multiple scholars argue that teachers must avoid fatalism and pursue new collaborative opportunities. Danaher, Gale, and Erben (2000) contend that teacher communities can challenge the individualism the marketization of higher education promotes. Harris (2005, 428) echoes this sentiment by saying that, 'We need to find ways of exchanging ideas and ways of working within and across disciplines and institutions which are underpinned by shared values and understandings about the moral purpose of working in academia'. Zhang (2009) goes a step further by asserting that, 'Sustained innovation and deep reform in education requires the development of innovative teacher communities' (277).

OERs and OTCNs

While teaching communities are not new, with the introduction of Web 2.0 technologies, teaching communities of every variety can form between teacher/scholars who may have never met before and most likely do not live in close proximity. Of all the online resources, media, and information about teaching, we can divide most of it across two types of offerings: OERs and OTCNs. OERs are digital repositories of educational ideas, activities, and other useful classroom content/media designed for reuse and repurposing (Atkins, Brown, and Hammond 2007; Veletsianos and Kimmons 2012). OTCNs, a term we are coining here, are avenues for educators to form collegial communities that provide support and informal mentoring. We should note that these are not mutually exclusive, but that the functions they serve are so disparate that to lump them together into a single category would be to give insufficient attention to aspects of each (e.g. the current literature gives far more attention to the resources available online than the communities forming). Furthermore, there are examples of each that would not fit underneath the opposite label; for instance an email listserv used for discussing classroom issues is not an aggregated resource collection, but rather a communication platform for a community. Antonio Martinez-Arboleda from Leeds University points out on the Jorum website that OERs like Jorum do not maintain a profile of users uploading their content. He points out that creating a profile for users 'would help to develop a stronger "sense of pedagogical community" around it'.

Before we go any further, it is important that we define the scope of our present discussion and situate it within the larger context of academic offerings online. The term open scholarship can be thought of as a broad umbrella term that includes OERs, academic blogs, and social media productions that are focused on all aspects of education including scholarship, research, and service at every level of education (i.e. primary to postsecondary education) (Veletsianos and Kimmons 2012). The networks of relationships that form around all of these online offerings (and that occasionally form independent of any other resource) represent the OTCNs discussed in this article.

Within this umbrella is a section focused primarily on higher education and within that subsection is an area focused primarily on pedagogy and teachers.

Open educational resources (OERs)

An OER is a curated digital repository of innovative approaches to learning, class activities, assignments, media, and other pedagogical content that is intended to be reused, repurposed, and redistributed at no cost by teachers or by students engaged in self-directed study (Support Center for Open Resources in Education website). OERs use Web 2.0 technologies, to create, catalog, and distribute their resources (Caswell et al. 2008). Weller (2011) suggests that we divide OERS between big and little OERs. The former are typically sponsored/funded by academic institutions, have clearly articulated pedagogical aims, and the quality of their offerings is more consistent. Little OERs, on the other hand, are often produced by a single academic, the resources are often of a low budget variety, and the quality of their offerings varies widely from one source to another.

Some have argued that the OER movement represents a proactive response to the trying times educators face:

> [The OER movement and the OERs it produces] are a direct response to the challenges and opportunities of a digital, networked, open approach in education. They may not be the solutions in themselves, and maybe several years from now they will be superseded, but they can be interpreted as generating feedback and experimenting with possibilities and alternatives that were previously unavailable. (Weller 2011)

Teaching innovations, activities, and assignments are less likely to be published in peer-reviewed journals and when the teaching resource is based on a current event, the time-consuming journal publication process prevents the distribution of the resource while it is most valuable (Bouwma-Gearhart and Bess 2012). Therefore, OERs are an important distribution channel as they can publish teaching resources journals cannot or would not and do so in a fraction of the time. However, we must acknowledge that these resources are not generally peer reviewed like their journal counterparts. That said, Street et al. (2012) find that a majority of contingent faculty do not have access to library resources or journal databases meaning that for all the virtue of peer-reviewed teaching resources, the majority of the educators who teach a majority of students are unable to use them.

OERs also differentiate from peer-reviewed journals in their focus on rapid collaboration and adaptation. The OER life cycle, as defined by Wiley (2007) is compose, adapt, use, and share. Educators who use OER resources are encouraged to copy, modify, and repurpose them both by the spirit of the OER movement and legally by the creative commons license that paves the way for each step of the life cycle.

OTCNs

Hunt, Mair, and Atkinson (2012, 199) coined the term TCNs to refer to a face-to-face, 'informal social network that exchanges teaching-specific resources, such as information and social support'. Research on teaching communities foster professional development and personal growth (Glowacki-Dudka and Brown 2007), enhance peer support, collegiality, critical companionship, collaboration, knowledge sharing and the benchmarking of practices (Sinclair and Levett-Jones 2011, 40), and promote innovation and creativity (Berlanga and Vuorikari 2012). Additionally, the social ties made through the community can help create normative cultures and distribute ideas, innovations, and opportunities across the network (i.e. social capital) (Bankston and Zhou 2002; Spalter-Roth et al. 2010).

Educators today can also turn online to meet many of the same needs that a traditional offline teaching community provides. As an example of an OTCN, many disciplines have email listservs or similar forums that are designed to help instructors get their questions answered, offer them a space to share their classroom experiences to an empathetic ear, and otherwise tap into the collective wisdom of their peers. Many of the same OTCN functions are carried out using Twitter, the comments sections on blogs, and nearly every other social media platform available.

OTCNs take place in settings that sometimes have formal rules (e.g. a private discipline specific email listserv) and sometimes have no formal rules (e.g. Twitter). Furthermore, OTCNs can form in places where fostering community is the intent of the space, but they can also organically spring up in places where fostering a teacher community network is not the expressed purpose (e.g. the comments below a YouTube video). The Internet as a medium is a decentralized, nonhierarchical, and unwieldy medium that is powerful precisely because it is a network of 'small pieces loosely joined' (Weinberger 2002); so it should surprise no one that OTCNs are scattered across the Web.

It is far easier to understand OERs and OTCNs by examining both within a single discipline. The teaching community that has formed within the discipline of sociology is an illustrative example of how pedagogy in higher education can be improved through collaboration online. In the following section we will describe the variety of OERs and OTCNs available to sociology educators to provide an example of an informal, decentralized, network of educators coming together.

OERs and OTCNs within sociology

Sociology as a discipline has a vibrant community of online public scholars and teachers who share their perspectives, resources, and ideas with peers and the general public. For those who teach sociology there are a wide variety of OERs and OTCNs to support them. The technology that undergirds the majority of sociology OERs is a blogging engine, but often they have been customized to perform more like a catalog of submissions from other teachers (e.g. SociologySounds.com). Even with blogs serving as the primary distribution method, many Sociology OERs use Facebook, Twitter, Pinterest, YouTube, and the like to also share their resources and to promote the formation of OTCNs (e.g. Sociological Images). While taken together the OERs and OTCNs can be best described as a loose network of individuals and small teams, we can see evidence of the interconnection every time an author links to another site within the community (Batts, Anthis, and Smith 2008).

Sociology OERs

For the purposes of this article we will divide all of the sociology OERs into four different types: blogs and OERs that are focused primarily on teaching sociology, general OERs that include sections on sociology, sociology blogs that are only tangentially focused on teaching, and sociology OERs created by textbook publishers.

Sites like *The Sociological Cinema* (thesociologicalcinema.com), Sociology-Source, (sociologysource.org), and *Teaching TSP* (thesocietypages.org/teaching) are OERs focused on delivering ideas and resources for teaching sociology. *The Sociological Cinema* curates a list of online videos from other sites (e.g. YouTube) that complement the topics often taught in sociology classes (Andrist, Chepp, and Dean 2011). The site also 'posts interactive blogs offering commentary, video recommendations, and research related to the efficacy of using film, multimedia, and other visual aids' (Caldeira and Ferrante 2012, 191). *SociologySource*, which in the spirit of full disclosure is written and edited by both the authors of this piece, has a broader approach, providing teachers with ideas, anecdotes from the classroom, and pedagogical resources (e.g. directions for assignments or class activities). *Teaching TSP* is a teaching focused site within the network of sociology blogs on thesocietypages.org. *Teaching TSP* highlights articles on *The Society Pages* that can be used in instruction and in addition they also have a collection of authors who post ideas and resources that are only published on *Teaching TSP*.

Many OERs are not focused on any particular subject, but are focused on the instruction across disciplines and include popular OERs such as Jorum (jorum.ac.uk/), OER Commons (oercommons.org/), MERLOT (merlot.org/merlot/index.htm), and Connexions (cnx.org/), just to name a few. These sites feature a wide variety of pedagogical resources for sociology instructors including teaching activities, lecture slides, and even an open source textbooks.

There is a much larger collection of sociology blogs that do not focus primarily on teaching, but occasionally discuss teaching and/or provide resources for instruction. This is probably best illustrated by the award winning website *Sociological Images* (thesocietypages.org/socimages); a blog where images from popular culture and scholarly research are sociologically analyzed. *Sociological Images* also provides teachers with assignments and course guides (i.e. collections of blog posts that fit with a particular sociological topic). Many teachers across the globe use *Sociological Images* in their classes, often as a springboard into class discussions (Mayeda, 2010; Wade and Sharp 2013).

Textbook publishers have also joined the OER movement with blogs that use pop culture and current events to illustrate sociological concepts. For example, *Everyday Sociology Blog* (everydaysociologyblog.com), which W.W. Norton & Company, Inc. owns, is a blog that according to their website, 'features interesting, informative, and most of all entertaining commentary from sociologists around the United States'. In addition, Pearson publishes the blog *SociologyInFocus* (sociologyinfocus.com), where the first author of this piece serves as editor-in-chief. The site 'takes a topic straight from the headlines, pop culture, or the media and uses it as an illustrative example of sociological concepts'.

Sociological OTCNs

The Teaching Sociology Google Group is perhaps the clearest example of the community building nature of OTCNs. Previously an email listserv, this Google

Group was created to provide an online platform for sociology educators to ask and answer each other's questions and share their ideas for teaching sociology. With 819 registered members (Email from Carolyn Pevey, 7 February 2013), this active OTCN provides educators everywhere with the opportunity to dialog with peers, brainstorm ideas, find solutions to common classroom issues, develop collegial friendships, and find mentoring.

While *The Sociological Cinema*'s main web page is a fairly standard OER for sharing online videos, they have a thriving community of teachers and fans of the site on their Facebook page (Facebook.com/pages/The-Sociological-Cinema/) with more than 40,000 'likes' (akin to subscribers). The page features links to web content focused on teaching/sociology, quotes that drive home sociological concepts, as well as videos and images (or what are known as memes) that challenge inequality/privilege. While it may be easy to dismiss this content as being nothing more than Internet fodder tailored to the interests of teachers and sociologists, this would discount the member discourse taking place in the comments section below each entry. Here educators engage one another in dialog and debate as well as provide informal support and critical feedback to one another. While *The Sociological Cinema's* Facebook presence is illustrative of OTCNs within sociology and perhaps the most frequently used OTCN, there are many other spaces where sociology OTCNs form.

Although the majority of interactions with the OTCN take place online, these collegial digital relationships have prompted offline face-to-face interactions at regional and national sociology conferences. For instance in 2012 at the American Sociological Association Conference in Denver, Colorado the authors, contributors, members, and readers of many of the leading sociology blogs (including *The Sociological Cinema* and *Sociological Images)* met in person to solidify collegial friendships and put a human face on the people they had been interacting with. Later that same day, sociology bloggers from a wide variety of subdisciplines and multiple countries met at what was dubbed the, '2012 Blog-Get-Together'. The desire to bring a community from an online space into the tangible world suggests that, at least for some, OTCNs serve similar functions as offline TCNs.

Possibilities and limitations

Both OERs and OTCNs represent significant developments within the global education system, but both have clear areas for improvement and limits on what they can offer. Currently very little is known about the OTCNs that form around, between, and outside of OERs. To be clear, there is some discussion of online communities, however limited, (Sun 2010; Tosato and Bodi 2012) and there is research on OERs that at least mentions community (Hylén 2006; Weller 2011; Masterman et al. 2011), but in almost every case the community aspects of OERs are only given a cursory examination. We here coined the term OTCNs in the hopes that naming the phenomenon will encourage scholars to begin exploring it as a separate phenomenon or at the very least an important aspect of OERs worthy of serious attention.

Within the OER movement there remain a series of hurdles to overcome if OERs are to maximize their potential. First, awareness of OERs has not yet achieved critical mass. We need established institutions like discipline associations and university systems to raise awareness by featuring OERs in their newsletters, on their websites, and through the rest of their communication channels. Second, OERS need to educate users on the fundamentals of sharing resources online; for instance research suggests that many OER users do not understand creative commons licensing (Masterman et al. 2011), which is the legal concept that undergirds the entire movement. Finally, at the present moment there are some pronounced technological competencies that users must obtain before OERs can be of use to them.

Similarly, one of the greatest strengths of OERs and OTCNs is that they are nonhierarchical and decentralized, but this may also be their greatest weakness. A large portion of the OERs available intermittently publish their offerings across a vast array of individual outlets. OTCNs by definition can take place anywhere on the Internet and often they form in places where the formation of teacher networks is not the expressed purpose of the platform (e.g. Twitter). Research is needed to assess if the decentralized (or as critics might put it, scattered) sources prevent many sociology educators from finding them in the first place. Hookway (2008, 107), when discussing blogs, makes a point that could be extended to all forms of social media, '[they] have their pitfalls and benefits. On the one hand, entering the blogosphere, with its endless maze of blogs and blog voices, can be a disorientating, time-consuming and overwhelming experience that only reluctantly yields relevant data'. The academic hierarchy may be exclusive, but it has much more developed mechanisms for disseminating its ideas and innovations.

Ultimately both OERs and OTCNs are focused on encouraging pedagogical innovation and subsequently increasing student learning. At present, we have no way of knowing empirically if pedagogy has been improved by OERs and/or OTCNs. We need research that evaluates how resources culled from the online teaching community affect student-learning gains.

Research is needed to contextualize the value OTCNs offer educators. Do educators at two-year institutions have different experiences than their counterparts at four-year schools? What differences are there between and across nations? Are faculty in the UK using OERs and OTCNs in manners different from how they are being used by faculty in China? Presently, there is no solid answer to these questions.

While we are discussing scholarship, we should note that much has been made about the differences between peer-reviewed scholarship and the pedagogy/scholarship happening online that is not peer reviewed. We join the scholars who have argued that the two need not be adversaries, but rather both stand to benefit from the other (Pearce et al. 2011, 6). Proponents of academic blogs argue that non-peer-reviewed blogs provide resources and opportunities that peer-reviewed journals cannot. While at the same time, it is also true that online teaching resources are not able to assess their impact directly. Here we are calling for the scholarship of teaching and learning to investigate the emerging online teaching community. Educators everywhere stand to benefit from a collaborative union between the two.

Conclusion

OERs and OTCNs represent a counter trend by faculty to the trying times they face. Both operate seamlessly within a marketization of higher education (Schejbal 2012, 1); while at the same time they challenge the traditional hierarchies within academia. Furthermore, these communities of passionate educators are, as Barnett (2010, 50) encouraged, ameliorating the pernicious aspects of marketization and heightening the virtuous.

As OERs and OTCNs play an increasing role in the work faculty do, they will be increasingly harder to ignore. As Hamlin (2010) argues we must prepare, 'to embrace new definitions of scholarship, knowledge, and the expression of the ways of seeing. Although the virtual world is not the antithesis of traditional forms of expression, it is clearly transforming the academic world' (362). OERs and OTCNs represent the best of what is possible when we operate outside of the academic hierarchy.

References

AFT Higher Education. 2009. *American Academic: The State of the Higher Education Workforce, 1997–2007*. American Federation of Teachers, AFL-CIO (AFT). http://www.aft.org/pdfs/highered/aa_highedworkforce0209.pdf.

American Association of University Professors. 2003. *Policy Statement: Contingent Appointments and the Academic Profession*. Washington, DC: American Association of University Professors. http://www.aaup.org/AAUP/pubsres/policydocs/contents/conting-stmt.htm.

Anderson, W. A., U. Banerjee, C. L. Drennan, S. C. R. Elgin, I. R. Epstein, J. Handelsman, G. F. Hatfull, et al. 2011. "Changing the Culture of Science Education at Research Universities." *Science* 331 (6014): 152–153. doi:10.1126/science.1198280.

Andrist, L., V. Chepp, and P. Dean. 2011. "Using Video in the Classroom: Pedagogy and the Sociological Cinema." *Teaching/Learning Matters* 39 (3): 8–10. http://webcache.googleusercontent.com/search?q=cache:Fz-NJBGkkFAJ:www2.asanet.org/sectionteach/v39n3.pdf+&cd=1&hl=en&ct=clnk&gl=us&client=firefox-a.

Arum, R., and J. Roska. 2011. *Academically Drift: Limited Learning on College Campuses*. Chicago: University of Chicago Press.

Atkins, D. E., J. S. Brown, and A. L. Hammond. 2007. *A Review of the Open Educational Resources (OER) Movement: Achievements, Challenges, and New Opportunities*. Report to The William and Flora Hewlett Foundation. San Francisco, CA: Creative Common. http://www.hewlett.org/uploads/files/ReviewoftheOERMovement.pdf.

Bankston, C. L., and M. Zhou. 2002. "Social Capital as Process: The Meanings and Problems of a Theoretical Metaphor." *Sociological Inquiry* 72 (2): 285–317. doi:10.1111/1475-682X.00017.

Barnett, R. 2010. "The Marketised University: Defending The Indefensible." In *The Marketization of Higher Education and the Student as Consumer*, edited by M. Molesworth, R. Scullion, and E. Nixon, 39–51. New York: Routledge.

Basken, P. 2011. "Scientists Fault Universities as Favoring Research Over Teaching." *The Chronicle of Higher Education*, January 13. http://chronicle.com/article/Scientists-Fault-Universities/125944/.

Batts, S. A., N. J. Anthis, and T. C. Smith. 2008. "Advancing Science Through Conversations: Bridging the Gap between Blogs and the Academy." *PLoS Biology* 6 (9): e240. doi:10.1371/journal.pbio.0060240.

Berlanga, A., and R. Vuorikari. 2012. "Symposium: Learning Networks for Professional Development: Current Research Approaches and Future Trends." In *Proceedings of the Eighth International Conference of Networked Learning*, edited by V. Hodgson, C. Jones, M. ed Laat, D. McConnell, T. Ryberg, and P. Sloep, 412–413. April 2–4, 2012, Maastricht: Creative Common. http://hdl.handle.net/1820/4226.

Bossu, C., and B. Tynan. 2011. "OERs: New Media on the Learning Landscape." *On the Horizon* 19 (4): 259–267. doi:10.1108/10748121111179385.

Bouwma-Gearhart, J. L., and J. L. Bess. 2012. "The Transformative Potential of Blogs for Research in Higher Education." *The Journal of Higher Education* 83 (2): 249–275. doi:10.1353/jhe.2012.0008.

Caldeira, C., and J. Ferrante. 2012. "The Sociological Cinema: Teaching and Learning Sociology Through Video." *Teaching Sociology* 40 (2): 191–193. doi:10.1177/0092055X12439856.

Caswell, T., S. Henson, M. Jensen, and D. Wiley. 2008. "Open Content and Open Educational Resources: Enabling Universal Education." *The International Review of Research in Open*

and Distance Learning 9 (1): 1–7. http://www.irrodl.org/index.php/irrodl/article/view/469/1001.
Danaher, P. A., T. Gale, and T. Erben. 2000. "The Teacher Educator as (Re)Negotiated Professional: Critical Incidents in Steering between State and Market in Australia." *Journal of Education for Teaching* 26 (1): 55–71. doi:10.1080/02607470050007138.
Deem, R. 1998. "'New Managerialism' and Higher Education: The Management of Performances and Cultures in Universities in the United Kingdom." *International Studies in Sociology of Education* 8 (1): 47–70. doi:10.1080/0962021980020014.
Eurostat. 2010. "Education and Training Statistics." European Commission. Accessed February 3. http://www.epp.eurostat.ec.europa.eu/portal/page/portal/education/data/database.
Ginsberg, B. 2011. *Fall of the Faculty: The Rise of the All-administrative University and Why it Matters*. New York: Oxford University Press.
Glowacki-Dudka, M., and M. P. Brown. 2007. "Professional Development Through Faculty Learning Communities." *New Horizons in Adult Education and Human Resource Development* 21 (1/2): 29–39. doi:10.1002/nha3.10277.
Hamlin, J. 2010. "Epistemology, Pedagogy, and Latent Functions: The Peculiar Nature of Web-based Public Access Courses." *International Journal of Teaching and Learning in Higher Education* 22 (3): 357–364. http://www.isetl.org/ijtlhe/.
Harris, S. 2005. "Rethinking Academic Identities in Neo-liberal Times." *Teaching in Higher Education* 10 (4): 421–433. doi:10.1080/13562510500238986.
Hookway, N. 2008. "Entering the Blogosphere: Some Strategies for Using Blogs in Social Research." *Qualitative Research* 8 (1): 91–113. doi:10.1177/1468794107085298.
Hung, H. T., and S. C. Yuen. 2010. "Educational Use of Social Networking Technology in Higher Education." *Teaching in Higher Education* 15 (6): 703–714. doi:10.1080/13562517.2010.507307.
Hunt, A. N., C. A. Mair, and M. P. Atkinson. 2012. "Teaching Community Networks: A Case Study of Informal Social Support and Information Sharing among Sociology Graduate Students." *Teaching Sociology* 40 (3): 198–214. doi:10.1177/0092055X12441714.
Hylén, J. 2006. "Open Educational Resources: Opportunities and Challenges." *Proceedings of Open Education* 49–63. Accessed February 3. http://www.knowledgeall.net/files/Additional_Readings-Consolidated.pdf.
Kezar, A., and C. Sam. 2010. "Non-Tenure-Track Faculty in Higher Education: Theories and Tensions. *ASHE Higher Education Report* 36 (5): 1–91. doi:10.1002/aehe.3605.
Macdonald, I. 2001. "The Teaching Community: Recreating University Teaching." *Teaching in Higher Education* 6 (2): 153–167. doi:10.1080/13562510120045168.
Masterman, L., J. Wild, D. White, J. Wild, L. Masterman, and M. Manton. 2011. *JISC Open Educational Resources Programme: Phase 2 OER Impact Study: Research Report*. Mountain View: Creative Common, University of Oxford.
Mayeda, D. T. 2010. "Film Review: Sociological Images: Inspiring Sociological Imaginations Everywhere." *Teaching Sociology* 38 (4): 401–403. doi:10.1177/0092055X10380851.
Molesworth, M., E. Nixon, and R. Scullion. 2009. "Having, Being and Higher Education: The Marketisation of the University and the Transformation of the Student into Consumer." *Teaching in Higher Education* 14 (3): 277–287. doi:10.1080/13562510902898841.
Monks, J., and R. Schmidt. 2010. *The Impact of Class Size on Outcomes in Higher Education*. Cornell Higher Education Research Institute, Cornell University, School of Industrial and Labor Relations. http://digitalcommons.ilr.cornell.edu/workingpapers/114/.
Nickolai, D. H., S. G. Hoffman, and M. N. Trautner. 2012. "Can a Knowledge Sanctuary Also Be an Economic Engine? The Marketization of Higher Education as Institutional Boundary Work." *Sociology Compass* 6 (3): 205–218. doi:10.1111/j.1751-9020.2011.00449.x.
Oplatka, I., and J. Hemsley-Brown. 2010. "The Globalization and Marketization of Higher Education: Some Insights From the Standpoint of Institutional Theory." In *Globalization and Internationalization in Higher Education: Theoretical, Strategic and Management Perspectives*, edited by F. Maringe and N. Foskett, 65–80. New York, NY and London: Continuum International Publishing Group.
Pearce, N., M. Weller, E. Scanlon, and S. Kinsley. 2011. "Digital Scholarship Considered: How New Technologies Could Transform Academic Work." *In Education* 16 (1): 33–44.

http://www.ineducation.ca/article/digital-scholarship-considered-how-new-technologies-could-transform-academic-work.

Schejbal, D. 2012. "In Search of a New Paradigm for Higher Education." *Innovative Higher Education* 38 (1): 1–14. doi:10.1007/s10755-012-9218-z.

Schrecker, E. 2010. *The Lost Soul of Higher Education: Corporatization, the Assault on Academic Freedom, and the End of the American University.* New York, NY: The New Press.

Schuster, J. H. 2011. "The Professoriate's Perilous Path." In *The American Academic Profession: Transformation in Contemporary Higher Education*, edited by J. C. Hermanowicz, 1–20. Baltimore: The John Hopkins University Press.

Sinclair, P. M., and T. Levett-Jones. 2011. "The Evolution of the Nephrology Educators' Network." *Journal of Renal Care* 37 (1): 40–46. doi:10.1111/j.1755-6686.2011.00208.x.

Spalter-Roth, R., O. Mayorova, J. Scelza, and N. Van Vooren. 2010. *Teaching Alone? Sociology Faculty and the Availability of Social Networks.* Washington, DC: American Sociological Association. http://www.asanet.org/images/research/docs/pdf/NetworkBrief1_Jun10.pdf.

Street, S., M. Maisto, E. Merves, and G. Rhoades. 2012. "Who Is Professor "Staff": And How Can This Person Teach so Many Classes." Center for the Future of Higher Education Policy Report #2. http://www.google.com/url?sa=t&rct=j&q=&esrc=s&source=web&cd=1&ved=0CCsQFjAA&url=http%3A%2F%2Fwww.insidehighered.com%2Fsites%2Fdefault%2Fserver_files%2Ffiles%2Fprofstaff%282%29.pdf&ei=paYjUoi2LoGriAKc-oH4CQ&usg=AFQjCNGu8D-MX32ShkYZJ9zeNHGY_ckiJA&sig2=c0OoZyYhfDfBXNpO2WMcUA&bvm=bv.51495398,d.cGE

Sun, Y.-C. 2010. "Developing Reflective Cyber Communities in the Blogosphere: A Case Study in Taiwan Higher Education." *Teaching in Higher Education* 15 (4): 369–381. doi:10.1080/13562510903556075.

Tan, E., and N. Pearce. 2012. "Open Education Videos in the Classroom: Exploring the Opportunities and Barriers to the Use of YouTube in Teaching Introductory Sociology." ALT-C 2011 Proceedings Papers, Association for Learning Technology. http://repository.alt.ac.uk/2181/7/RLT_A_007783_O.html.

Thelin, J. R. 2011. *A History of American Higher Education.* 2nd ed. Baltimore: The Johns Hopkins University Press.

Tosato, P., and G. Bodi. 2012. "Collaborative Environments to Foster Creativity, Reuse and Sharing of OER." *The European Journal of Open, Distance and E-Learning*. http://www.eurodl.org/index.php.

Veletsianos, G., and R. Kimmons. 2012. "Assumptions and Challenges of Open Scholarship." *The International Review of Research in Open and Distance Learning* 13 (4): 166–189. http://www.irrodl.org/index.php/irrodl/article/view/1313/2304.

Wade L., and G. Sharp. 2013. "Sociological Images: Blogging as Public Sociology." *Social Science Computer Review* 31 (4): 221–228. doi:10.1177/0894439312442356.

Weinberger, D. 2002. *Small Pieces Loosely Joined: A Unified Theory of the Web.* Basic Books.

Weller, M. 2011. *The Digital Scholar: How Technology is Transforming Scholarly Practice.* London, UK: Bloomsbury Academic.

Wiley, D. 2007. "Open Educational Resources: On the Sustainability of OER initiatives in Higher Education." Paper commissioned by the OECD's Centre for Educational Research and Innovation (CERI) for the project on Open Educational Resources. http://www.oecd.org/dataoecd/33/9/38645447.pdf.

Xiong, T. 2012. "Discourse and Marketization of Higher Education in China: The Genre of Advertisements for Academic Posts." *Discourse & Society* 23 (3): 318–337. doi:10.1177/0957926511433786.

Zhang, J. 2009. "Comments on Greenhow, Robelia, and Hughes: Toward a Creative Social Web for Learners and Teachers." *Educational Researcher* 38 (4): 274–279. doi:10.3102/0013189X09336674.

Index

Page references for tables are bold; page references for figures are italic.